T0253971

Full Stack JavaScript

Learn Backbone.js, Node.js and MongoDB

Second Edition

Azat Mardan

Apress®

Full Stack JavaScript: Learn Backbone.js, Node.js and MongoDB

Copyright © 2016 by Azat Mardan

This work is subject to copyright. All rights are reserved by the Publisher, whether the whole or part of the material is concerned, specifically the rights of translation, reprinting, reuse of illustrations, recitation, broadcasting, reproduction on microfilms or in any other physical way, and transmission or information storage and retrieval, electronic adaptation, computer software, or by similar or dissimilar methodology now known or hereafter developed. Exempted from this legal reservation are brief excerpts in connection with reviews or scholarly analysis or material supplied specifically for the purpose of being entered and executed on a computer system, for exclusive use by the purchaser of the work. Duplication of this publication or parts thereof is permitted only under the provisions of the Copyright Law of the Publisher's location, in its current version, and permission for use must always be obtained from Springer. Permissions for use may be obtained through RightsLink at the Copyright Clearance Center. Violations are liable to prosecution under the respective Copyright Law.

ISBN-13 (pbk): 978-1-4842-1750-4

ISBN-13 (electronic): 978-1-4842-1751-1

Trademarked names, logos, and images may appear in this book. Rather than use a trademark symbol with every occurrence of a trademarked name, logo, or image we use the names, logos, and images only in an editorial fashion and to the benefit of the trademark owner, with no intention of infringement of the trademark.

The use in this publication of trade names, trademarks, service marks, and similar terms, even if they are not identified as such, is not to be taken as an expression of opinion as to whether or not they are subject to proprietary rights.

While the advice and information in this book are believed to be true and accurate at the date of publication, neither the authors nor the editors nor the publisher can accept any legal responsibility for any errors or omissions that may be made. The publisher makes no warranty, express or implied, with respect to the material contained herein.

Managing Director: Welmoed Spahr
Lead Editor: Jeffrey Pepper
Editorial Board: Steve Anglin, Pramila Balan, Louise Corrigan, Jonathan Gennick,
    Robert Hutchinson, Celestin Suresh John, Michelle Lowman, James Markham,
    Susan McDermott, Matthew Moodie, Jeffrey Pepper, Douglas Pundick,
    Ben Renow-Clarke, Gwenan Spearing
Coordinating Editor: Mark Powers
Copy Editors: Teresa Horton and Karen Jameson
Compositor: SPi Global
Indexer: SPi Global
Artist: SPi Global

Distributed to the book trade worldwide by Springer Science+Business Media New York, 233 Spring Street, 6th Floor, New York, NY 10013. Phone 1-800-SPRINGER, fax (201) 348-4505, e-mail orders-ny@springer-sbm.com, or visit www.springeronline.com. Apress Media, LLC is a California LLC and the sole member (owner) is Springer Science + Business Media Finance Inc (SSBM Finance Inc). SSBM Finance Inc is a Delaware corporation.

For information on translations, please e-mail rights@apress.com, or visit www.apress.com.

Apress and friends of ED books may be purchased in bulk for academic, corporate, or promotional use. eBook versions and licenses are also available for most titles. For more information, reference our Special Bulk Sales–eBook Licensing web page at www.apress.com/bulk-sales.

Any source code or other supplementary materials referenced by the author in this text is available to readers at www.apress.com/9781484217504. For detailed information about how to locate your book's source code, go to www.apress.com/source-code/. Readers can also access source code at SpringerLink in the Supplementary Material section for each chapter.

To my parents, Almas and Alsu, who bought me my first computer, and let me use the phone line for dial-up Internet

Contents at a Glance

Contents

About the Author

Azat Mardan has over 14 years of experience in web, mobile, and software development. With a Bachelor's degree in Informatics and a Master of Science degree in Information Systems Technology, Azat possesses deep academic knowledge as well as extensive practical experience. Azat is an experienced software engineer, author and educator. He has published 11 books and counting.

Currently, Azat works as a Technology Fellow at Capital One Financial Corporation, a technology company with a focus on finance. Before that, Azat was a Team Lead at DocuSign, where his team rebuilt 50 million user products (DocuSign web app) using the tech stack of Node.js, Express.js, Backbone.js, CoffeeScript, Jade, Stylus, and Redis.

Recently, he worked as an engineer at the curated social media news aggregator web site, Storify.com (acquired by LiveFyre), which is used by BBC, NBC, CNN, the White House, and others. Storify runs everything on Node.js unlike other companies. It's the maintainer of the open source library jade browser.

Before that, Azat worked as a CTO/Cofounder at Gizmo—an enterprise cloud platform for mobile marketing campaigns, and has undertaken the prestigious 500 Startups business accelerator program.

Prior to this, Azat was developing the developed mission-critical applications for government agencies in Washington, DC, including the National Institutes of Health, the National Center for Biotechnology Information, and the Federal Deposit Insurance Corporation, as well as Lockheed Martin.

Azat is a frequent attendee at Bay Area tech meet-ups and hackathons (AngelHack hackathon '12 finalist with team FashionMetric.com, which went on to raise venture capital from Mark Cuban and TechStars).

In addition, Azat teaches technical classes at General Assembly, Hack Reactor, pariSOMA, and Marakana (acquired by Twitter) to much acclaim.

In his spare time, he writes about technology on his blog: Webapplog.com, which was a number one in "express.js tutorial" Google search results for some time.

Azat is also the author of *Pro Express.js, Practical Node.js and Node Program*, and others. Azat is the creator of open source Node.js projects, including ExpressWorks, mongoui, and HackHall.

You can reach Azat and say hi using one of these methods:

Twitter: [@azat_co](https://twitter.com/azat_co) - Azat loves getting "Hi" on Twitter

Facebook

Blog: webapplog.com

GitHub: github.com/azat-co/fullstack-javascript

Share on Twitter

Tweet "I'm starting FullStack JavaScript by @azat_co @Apress " by opening this link http://ctt.ec/he3Ug.

Acknowledgments

I would like to thank the team of early Node contributors bringing JavaScript to the servers. Without them, the full stack JavaScript development wouldn't be possible.

I'm grateful to my copy and content editors at Apress specifially to James Markham, Mark Powers, Teresa Horton, and Karen Jameson. They accomplished an amazing feat by bringing this book to life in a span of a few weeks.

Also, I'm grateful to the students of Hack Reactor, Marakana, pariSOMA, and General Assembly where I taught and used early Full Stack JavaScript (or its parts) training material.

Preface

I'm writing this as I'm sitting at the San Francisco airport waiting for my flight to Portland, Oregon, for the biggest Node.js conference. I'll be speaking there about Node.js. It's scary and funny at the same time to think that I started to learn Node only three years ago. Yes, I remember how I decided that the best way to learn is to teach others. For this reason I started teaching my first Node classes and writing this book. The book was mostly for me, so I could remember how to push Heroku or how to create Node servers that talk to MongoDB. It was called Rapid Prototyping with JS back then. Three years sped away; I published a few more Node books as well as released several Node apps in production; and a few months ago Apress approached me wanting to publish an updated edition under a new title.

The main reason I bet my time and energy on JavaScript and Node in the first place is that I felt both intuitively and logically the potential of the full stack JavaScript. The one language to rule the whole stack across all the layers. Logically I understood the code reuse, expressiveness, and performance advantages of Node.js and the ever-increasing importance of front-end development with MVC-like frameworks such as Backbone. Intuitively, I just freaking fell in love with JavaScript both on the browser and on the server.

Yes, I used JavaScript for many years but it was more pain than fun. Not anymore. I was able to get a sense of what's going on at the front end while at the same time getting all the power and flexibility on the server. My brain started to think 5, maybe 10 times faster than before because I started to remember all the obscure methods from Array or String objects. I stopped having Mozilla Developer Network or Google open next to my code editor. And what a relief when you don't need to wait for the compiler each time that you want to test something really quickly.

The airline crew announced my boarding. I need to get on the plane, but I hope this easy, beginner-friendly manual will open the world of full stack JavaScript and cloud computing. Jump on the train of this amazing technology with me.

Introduction

The kind of programming that C provides will probably remain similar absolutely or slowly decline in usage, but relatively, JavaScript or its variants, or XML, will continue to become more central.

—Dennis Ritchie

In this chapter, we cover:

- Reasons behind full stack JavaScript development in general and for the writing of this book;

- Answers to questions what to expect and what not, what are prerequisites;

- Suggestions on how to use the book and examples;

- Explanation of the book's notation format.

Full Stack JavaScript is a hands-on book that introduces you to rapid software prototyping using the latest cutting-edge web and mobile technologies including Node.js, MongoDB, Twitter Bootstrap, LESS, jQuery, Parse.com, Heroku, and others.

Why This Book?

This book was borne out of frustration. I have been in software engineering for many years, and when I started learning Node.js and Backbone.js, I learned the hard way that their official documentation and the Internet lack in quick start guides and examples. Needless to say, it was virtually impossible to find all of the tutorials for JS-related modern technologies in one place.

The best way to learn is to do, right? Therefore, I've used the approach of small simple examples, that is, quick start guides, to expose myself to the new cool tech. After I was done with the basic apps, I needed some references and organization. I started to write this manual mostly for myself, so I can understand the concepts better and refer to the samples later. Then StartupMonthly and I taught a few two-day intensive classes on the same subject—helping experienced developers to jump start their careers with only-one-language development, that is, JavaScript. The manual we used was updated and iterated many times based on the feedback received. The end result is this book.

Why Go Full Stack JavaScript?

The reasons I love developing with full stack JavaScript, or as others call it universal or isomorphic JavaScript, are numerous:

- Code reuse: I can share my libraries, templates, and models between the browser and the server

- No context switch: my brain learns and thinks faster leaving me more time to work on the actual tasks at hand

- Great ecosystem: npm!

- Vibrant community: people who are eager to help and not all closed up

- Great masters: treasure chest of knowledge and best practices accumulated through the years of browser JavaScript

- Tons of tutorials and good books: JavaScript is the most popular language, hence more people writing about it

- No compilation: development is faster with interpreted platforms

- Good performance: Node's non-blocking I/O is fast

- Evolving Standard: EMCA is pushing new and better version of JavaScript

I'm sure I've missed a few points, but you got the idea. Whatever the drawbacks of ES5 (the language most of us know as JavaScript) are, they are getting fixes in ES6/ES2015 and newer versions. The future for JavaScript is so bright we all will have to code with sunglasses on.

What to Expect

A typical reader of *Full Stack JavaScript* should expect a collection of quick start guides, tutorials, and suggestions (e.g., Git workflow). There is a lot of coding and not much theory. All the theory we cover is directly related to some of the practical aspects and is essential for better understanding of technologies and specific approaches in dealing with them, for example, JSONP and cross-domain calls.

In addition to coding examples, the book covers virtually all setup and deployment step by step.

You'll learn on the examples of Chat web/mobile applications starting with front-end components. There are a few versions of these applications, but by the end we'll put front end and back end together and deploy to the production environment. The Chat application contains all of the necessary components typical for a basic web app and will give you enough confidence to continue developing on your own, apply for a job/promotion, or build a startup!

Who This Book Is For

The book is designed for advanced-beginner and intermediate-level web and mobile developers: somebody who has been (or still is) an expert in other languages like Ruby on Rails, PHP, Perl, Python, or/and Java. The type of a developer who quickly wants to learn more about JavaScript and Node.js-related techniques for building web and mobile application prototypes. Our target user doesn't have time to dig through voluminous (or tiny, at the other extreme) official documentation. The goal of Full Stack JavaScript is not to make an expert out of a reader, but to help him/her to start building apps as soon as possible.

Full Stack JavaScript: Learn Backbone.js, Node.js and MongoDB, as you can tell from the name, is about taking your idea to a functional prototype in the form of a web or a mobile application as fast as possible. This thinking adheres to the Lean Startup methodology; therefore, this book would be more valuable to startup founders, but big companies' employees might also find it useful, especially if they plan to add new skills to their resumes.

What This Book Is Not

Full Stack JavaScript is neither a comprehensive book on several frameworks, libraries, or technologies (or just a particular one), nor a reference for all the tips and tricks of web development. Examples similar to ones in this book might be publicly available online.

Even more so, if you're not familiar with fundamental programming concepts like loops, if/else statements, arrays, hashes, object and functions, you won't find them in Full Stack JavaScript. Additionally, it would be challenging to follow our examples.

Many volumes of great books have been written on fundamental topics — the list of such resources is at the end of the book in the chapter "Further Reading." The purpose of Full Stack JavaScript is to give agile tools without replicating theory of programming and computer science.

Prerequisites

We recommend the following things to get the full advantage of the examples and materials covered:

- Knowledge of the fundamental programming concepts such as objects, functions, data structures (arrays, hashes), loops (for, while), conditions (if/else, switch)

- Basic web development skills including, but not limited to, HTML and CSS

- Mac OS X or UNIX/Linux systems are highly recommended for this book's examples and for web development in general, although it's still possible to hack your way on a Windows-based system

- Access to the Internet

- 5-20 hours of time

- Some cloud services require users' credit/debit card information even for free accounts

How to Use the Book

The digital version of this book comes in three formats:

1. PDF: suited for printing; opens in Adobe Reader, Mac OS X Preview, iOS apps, and other PDF viewers.

2. ePub: suited for iBook app on iPad and other iOS devices; to copy to devices use iTunes, Dropbox or e-mail to yourself.

3. mobi: suited for Kindles of all generations as well as desktop and mobile Amazon Kindle apps and Amazon Cloud Reader; to copy to devices use Whispernet, USB cable, or e-mail to yourself.

The links are either spelled out in parenthesis or provided in the footnotes. In the PDF version and other digital versions like Mobi for Kindle, the table of contents has local hyperlinks that allow you to jump to any part or chapter of the book. This is very useful for referring to certain parts of content later, e.g., if you want to look up how to deploy to Heroku, you can quickly jump to the needed commands.

I encourage you to take notes and highlight text as you read it studiously. It will improve the retention of the material.

There are summaries in the beginning of each chapter describing in a few short sentences what examples and topics the particular chapter covers.

Each project comes with a YouTube screencast video. I recommend reading and watching the videos to improve the comprehension. You can watch the videos first or read the text first. The videos are supplemental, so it's not a big deal if you are reading digital book offline or a print book, and don't have the ability to watch the video. The text covers everything there's in the videos. The reason why I recorded the screencast is because people learn differently; some prefer text and other videos. This way, you can take advantage of both media as well as see certain development steps in action.

For faster navigation between parts, chapters, and sections of the book, please use the book's navigation pane, which is based on the Table of Contents (the screenshot is below).

The Table of Contents pane in the Mac OS X Preview app

Examples

All of the source code for examples used in this book is available in the book itself
for the most part, as well as at the book's apress.com product page (`www.apress.com/9781484217504`) and in a public GitHub repository (`github.com/azat-co/fullstack-javascript`). You can also download files as a ZIP archive or use Git to pull them. More
on how to install and use Git will be covered later in the book. The source code files, folder
structure, and deployment files are supposed to work locally and/or remotely on PaaS
solutions, that is, Windows Azure and Heroku, with minor or no modifications.

Source code that is in the book is technically limited by the platform to the width
of about 70 characters. We tried our best to preserve the best JavaScript and HTML
formatting styles, but from time to time you might see backslashes (\). There is nothing
wrong with the code. Backslashes are line escape characters, and if you copy-paste the
code into the editor, the example should work just fine. Please note that code in GitHub
and in the book might differ in formatting.

Last, let me (and others) know if you spot any bugs, by submitting an issue to GitHub! Please, don't send me bugs in an e-mail, because a public forum like GH Issue will help others, prevent duplicates, and keep everything organized.

Notation

This is what source code blocks look like:

```
var object = {};
object.name = "Bob";
```

Terminal commands have a similar look but start with a dollar sign or $:

```
$ git push origin heroku
$ cd /etc/
$ ls
```

Inline file names, path/folder names, quotes, and special words/names are italicized, while command names (e.g., mongod and emphasized words, such as Note, are bold.

Terms

For the purposes of this book, we're using some terms interchangeably. Depending on the context, they might not mean exactly the same thing. For example, function = method = call, attribute = property = member = key, value = variable, object = hash = class, list = array, framework = library = module.

Additionally, "full stack" is listed as fullstack within code snippets.

CHAPTER 1

Basics

I think everyone should learn how to program a computer, because it teaches you how to think. I view computer science as a liberal art, something everyone should learn to do.

—Steve Jobs

In this chapter, we'll cover these topics:

- Overview of HTML, CSS, and JavaScript syntaxes
- Brief introduction to Agile methodology
- Advantages of cloud computing, Node.js, and MongoDB
- Descriptions of HTTP requests/responses and RESTful API concepts

If you are an experienced web developer, I don't recommend it, but feel free to skip this chapter. It's important to brush up on the fundamental concepts before moving forward. Why? Maybe you have heard and are familiar with some terms, but wonder what they actually mean. Another good reason is that this chapter will cover the RESTful API in a very beginner-friendly manner. REST is used in virtually all modern web architectures, and we'll use it in the book a lot. There is one last reason: You'll look smart at a cocktail party or in front of your colleagues and your boss by acing the hodpodge of web acronyms.

Front-End Definitions

Front end is a term for browser applications. In some conversations, it could mean servers facing the requests first. However, for this book we assume that all front end is limited to the browser and mobile apps and their code.

Front-end development, or front-end web development, implies the usage of various technologies. Each of them individually is not too complex, but the sheer number of them makes beginners timid. For example, there are Cascading Style Sheets (CSS), Hypertext Markup Language (HTML), Extensible Markup Language (XML), JavaScript, JavaScript Object Notation (JSON), Uniform Resource Identifier (URI), Hypertext Transfer Protocol (HTTP), and many other abbreviations.

1

In addition to the low-level technologies, there are numerous frameworks, tools, and libraries; for example, jQuery, Backbone.js, Angular.js, Grunt, and so on. Please don't confuse front-end frameworks with back-end frameworks: The latter run on the server whereas the former run on the browser.

Front-end web development consists of these components:

1. HTML or templates that compile to HTML

2. Stylesheets to make HTML pretty

3. JavaScript to add interactivity or some business logic to the browser app

4. Some hosting (AWS, Apache, Heroku, etc.)

5. Build scripts to prepare code, manage dependencies, and do pretty much anything that's needed

6. Logic to connect to the server (typically via XHR requests and RESTful API)

Now you know what a job that has the title of front-end developer entails. The great payback to mastering this hodgepodge is the ability to express your creativity by building beautiful and useful apps.

Before we start building, let's cover a bird's-eye view of the web request cycle.

Web Request Cycle

This is important for someone very new to the web development. The whole World Wide Web or the Internet is about communication between clients and servers. This communication happens by sending requests and receiving responses. Typically browsers (the most popular web clients) send requests to servers. Behind the scenes, servers send their own requests to other servers. Those requests are similar to the browser requests. The language of requests and responses is HTTP(S). Let's explore the browser request in more details.

The web request consists of the following steps:

1. A user types a URL or follows a link in his or her browser (also called the client).

2. The browser makes an HTTP request to the server.

3. The server processes the request, and if there are any parameters in a query string or body of the request, it takes them into account.

4. The server updates, gets, and transforms data in the database.

5. The server responds with an HTTP response containing data in HTML, JSON, or other formats.

6. The browser receives the HTTP response.

7. The browser renders an HTTP response to the user in HTML or any other format (e.g., JPEG, XML, JSON).

Mobile applications act in the same manner as regular web sites, only instead of a browser there is a native app. Mobile apps (native or HTML5) are just another client. Other minor differences between mobile and web include data transfer limitation due to carrier bandwidth, smaller screens, and the more efficient use of local storage. Most likely you, my reader, are a web developer aspiring to use your web chops in mobile. With JavaScript and HTML5 it's possible, so it's worth covering web development closer.

Mobile Development

Is mobile going to overtake web and desktop platforms? Maybe. For now the mobile development field is extremely immature and new. It's good if you are a pioneer, but most of us are not. This is a bigger gap in tooling and libraries compared to web. The gap is closing. With HTML5, you can write once and reuse code on mobile. There are other approaches as well.

These are the approaches to mobile development, each with its own advantages and disadvantages:

1. *Native:* Native iOS, Android, Blackberry apps built with Objective-C and Java.

2. *Abstracted native:* Native apps built with JavaScript in Appcelerator (http://www.appcelerator.com), Xamarin, (https://xamarin.com), Smartface (http://www.smartface.io) React Native or similar tools, and then compiled into native Objective-C or Java.

3. *Responsive:* Mobile web sites tailored for smaller screens with responsive design, CSS frameworks like Twitter Bootstrap (http://twitter.github.io/bootstrap/) or Foundation (http://foundation.zurb.com/), regular CSS, or different templates. You might use some JavaScript frameworks for the development like Backbone.js, Angular.js, Ember.js, or React.js.

4. *Hybrid:* HTML5 apps that consist of HTML, CSS, and JavaScript, and are usually built with frameworks like Sencha Touch (http://www.sencha.com/products/touch), Trigger. io (https://trigger.io), JO (http://joapp.com), React Native (https://facebook.github.io/react-native), or Ionic (http://ionicframework.com) and then wrapped into a native app with PhoneGap (http://phonegap.com). As in the third approach, you probably will want to use a JavaScript framework for the development, such as Backbone.js, Angular. js, Ember.js, or React.js.

My personal favorites are the second and fourth approaches. The second approach doesn't require a different code base. A minimal viable product (MVP) can be built by just adding a single link to the CSS library. The fourth approach is more powerful and provides more scalable (in a development sence) UIs. This is better suited for complex apps. Code reuse between cross-platform mobile and web is easy because most of the times you're writing in JavaScript.

HyperText Markup Language

HTML is not a programming language in itself. It is a set of markup tags that describe the content and present it in a structured and formatted way. HTML tags consist of a tag name inside of the angle brackets (<>). In most cases, tags surround the content, with the end tag having forward slash before the tag name.

In this example, each line is an HTML element:

```
<h2>Overview of HTML</h2>
<div>HTML is a ...</div>
<link rel="stylesheet" type="text/css" href="style.css" />
```

An HTML document itself is an element of the <html> tag, and all other elements are children of that <html> tag:

```
<!DOCTYPE html>
<html lang="en">
  <head>
    <link rel="stylesheet" type="text/css" href="style.css" />
  </head>
  <body>
    <h2>Overview of HTML</h2>
    <p>HTML is a ...</p>
  </body>
</html>
```

There are different flavors and versions of HTML, such as DHTML, XHTML 1.0, XHTML 1.1, XHTML 2, HTML 4, and HTML 5. This article does a good job of explaining the differences: Misunderstanding Markup: XHTML 2/HTML 5 Comic Strip (http://coding.smashingmagazine.com/2009/07/29/misunderstanding-markup-xhtml-2-comic-strip/).

Any HTML element can have attributes. The most important of them are class, id, style, data-name, onclick, and other event attributes such as onmouseover, onkeyup, and so on.

class

The class attribute defines a class that is used for styling in CSS or Domain Object Model (DOM) manipulation; for example:

```
<p class="normal">...</p>
```

id

The id attribute defines an ID that is similar in purpose to element class, but it has to be unique; for example:

```
<div id="footer">...</div>
```

style

The style attribute defines inline CSS to style an element; for example:

```
<font style="font-size:20px">...</font>
```

title

The title attribute specifies additional information that is usually presented in tooltips by most browsers; for example:

```
<a title="Up-vote the answer">...</a>
```

data-name

The data-name attribute allows for metadata to be stored in the DOM; for example:

```
<tr data-token="fa10a70c-21ca-4e73-aaf5-d889c7263a0e">...</tr>
```

onclick

The onclick attribute calls inline JavaScript code when a click event happens; for example:

```
<input type="button" onclick="validateForm();">...</a>
```

onmouseover

The onmouseover attribute is similar to onclick but for mouse hover events; for example:

```
<a onmouseover="javascript: this.setAttribute('css','color:red')">...</a>
```

Other HTML element attributes for inline JavaScript code are as follows:

- onfocus: When the browser focuses on an element
- onblur: When the browser focus leaves an element
- onkeydown: When a user presses a keyboard key
- ondblclick: When a user double-clicks the mouse
- onmousedown: When a user presses a mouse button
- onmouseup: When a user releases a mouse button
- onmouseout: When a user moves mouse out of the element area
- oncontextmenu: When a user opens a context menu

The full list of such events and a browser compatibility table are presented in Event compatibility tables (http://www.quirksmode.org/dom/events/index.html).

We'll use classes extensively with Twitter Bootstrap framework, but the use of inline CSS and JavaScript code is generally a bad idea, so we'll try to avoid it. However, it's good to know the names of the JavaScript events because they are used all over the place in jQuery, Backbone.js, and, of course, plain JavaScript. To convert the list of attributes to a list of JS events, just remove the prefixes on; for example, onclick attribute means click event.

More information is available at Example: Catching a mouse click (https://developer.mozilla.org/en-US/docs/JavaScript/Getting_Started#Example:_Catching_a_mouse_click), Wikipedia (http://en.wikipedia.org/wiki/HTML) and MDN (https://developer.mozilla.org/en-US/docs/Web/HTML).

Cascading Style Sheets

CSS provides a way to format and present content. An HTML document can have an external stylesheet included in it by a <link> tag, as shown in the previous examples, or it can have CSS code directly inside of a <style> tag:

```
<style>
  body {
    padding-top: 60px; /* 60px to make some space */
  }
</style>
```

Each HTML element can have id attributes, class attributes, or both:

```
<div id="main" class="large">
  Lorem ipsum dolor sit amet,
  Duis sit amet neque eu.
</div>
```

In CSS we access elements by their id, class, tag name, and in some edge cases, by parent–child relationships or element attribute value.

This sets the color of all the paragraphs (<p> tag) to gray (#999999):

```
p {
  color: #999999;
}
```

This sets padding of a <div> element with the id attribute of main:

```
div#main {
  padding-bottom: 2em;
  padding-top: 3em;
}
```

This sets the font size to 14 pixels for all elements with a class large:

```
.large {
  font-size: 14pt;
}
```

This hides <div>, which are direct children of the <body> element:

```
body > div {
  display: none;
}
```

This sets the width to 150 pixels for input which the name attribute is email:

```
input[name="email"] {
  width: 150px;
}
```

More information is available at Wikipedia (http://en.wikipedia.org/wiki/Cascading_Style_Sheets) and MDN (https://developer.mozilla.org/en-US/docs/Web/CSS).

CSS3 is an upgrade to CSS that includes new ways of doing things such as rounded corners, borders, and gradients, which were possible in regular CSS only with the help of PNG/GIF images and by using other tricks.

For more information refer to CSS3.info (http://css3.info), w3school (http://www.w3schools.com/css3/default.asp), and CSS3 vs. CSS comparison article on Smashing (http://coding.smashingmagazine.com/2011/04/21/css3-vs-css-a-speed-benchmark).

JavaScript

JavaScript (JS) was started in 1995 at Netscape as LiveScript. It has the same relationship with Java as a hamster has with a ham, so please don't confuse one with another.

These days, JavaScript is used for both client-side and server-side web, as well as in desktop application development, drones, Internet of Things (IoT), and other things. This is the main focus of this book because with JavaScript you can develop across all the layers. You don't need any other languages!

Let's start with JavaScript in HTML. Putting JS code into a <script> tag is the easiest way to use JavaScript in an HTML document:

```
<script type="text/javascript" language="javascript">
  alert("Hello world!")
  //simple alert dialog window
</script>
```

Be advised that mixing HTML and JS code is not a good idea, so to separate them we can move the code to an external file, and include it by setting source attribute src="filename.js" on script tag, for example, for the app.js resource:

```
<script src="js/app.js" type="text/javascript" language="javascript">
</script>
```

Note that the closing </script> tag is mandatory even with an empty element like we have where we include the external source file. Type and language attributes over the years became optional in modern browsers due to the overwhelming dominance of JavaScript.

Other ways to run JavaScript include the following:

- The inline approach already covered

- WebKit browser Developer Tools and FireBug consoles

- The interactive Node.js shell

One of the advantages of the JavaScript language is that it's loosely typed. This loose or weak typing, as opposed to strong typing (http://en.wikipedia.org/wiki/Strong_typing) in languages like C and Java, makes JavaScript a better programming language for prototyping. Here are some of the main types of JavaScript objects or classes (there are not classes per se; objects inherit from objects).

Number Primitives

Number primitives are numerical values; for example:

```
var num = 1
```

Number Object

This is the Number (https://developer.mozilla.org/en-US/docs/JavaScript/Reference/Global_Objects/Number) object and its methods; for example:

```
var numObj = new Number('123') //Number object
var num = numObj.valueOf()     //number primitive
var numStr = numObj.toString() //string representation
```

String Primitives

String primitives are sequences of characters inside of single or double quotes; for example:

```
var str = 'some string'
var newStr = "abcde".substr(1,2)
```

For convenience, JavaScript automatically wraps string primitives with String object methods, but they are not quite the same (https://developer.mozilla.org/en-US/docs/JavaScript/Reference/Global_Objects/String#Distinction_between_string_primitives_and_String_objects).

String Object

The String object has a lot of useful methods, like length, match, and so on; for example:

```
var strObj = new String("abcde") //String object
var str = strObj.valueOf()        //string primitive
strObj.match(/ab/)
str.match(/ab/) //both call will work
```

RegExp Object

Regular Expressions or RegExps are patterns of characters used in finding matches, replacing, and testing of strings.

```
var pattern = /[A-Z]+/
'ab'.match(pattern) // null
'AB'.match(pattern) // ["AB"]
```

The match() method returns an array of matches (["AB"]). If all you need is a Boolean true/false, then simply use pattern.test(str). For example:

```
var str = 'A'
var pattern = /[A-Z]+/
pattern.test(str) // true
```

Special Types

When in doubt (when debugging), you can always call typeof obj. Here are some of the special types used in JS:

- NaN: Not a number

- null: Null, nada, zip

- undefined: Undeclared variable

- function: Function

JSON

The JSON library allows us to parse and serialize JavaScript objects; for example:

```
var obj = JSON.parse('{a: 1, b: "hi"}')
var stringObj = JSON.stringify({a: 1, b: 'hi'})
```

Array Object

Arrays (https://developer.mozilla.org/en-US/docs/JavaScript/Reference/Global_Objects/Array) are zero-index-based lists. For example, to create an array:

```
var arr = new Array()
var arr = ['apple', 'orange', 'kiwi']
```

The Array object has a lot of nice methods, like indexOf, slice, and join. Make sure that you're familiar with them, because if used correctly, they'll save a lot of time.

Data Object

```
var obj = {name: 'Gala', url: 'img/gala100x100.jpg', price: 129}
```

or

```
var obj = new Object()
```

We provide more on inheritance patterns later.

Boolean Primitives and Objects

Just as with String and Number, Boolean (https://developer.mozilla.org/en-US/docs/JavaScript/Reference/Global_Objects/Boolean) can be a primitive and an object.

```
var bool1 = true
var bool2 = false
var boolObj = new Boolean(false)
```

Date Object

Date (https://developer.mozilla.org/en-US/docs/JavaScript/Reference/Global_Objects/Date) objects allow us to work with dates and time; for example:

```
var timestamp = Date.now() // 1368407802561
var d = new Date()         // Sun May 12 2013 18:17:11 GMT-0700 (PDT)
```

Math Object

These are used for mathematical constants and functions (https://developer.mozilla.org/en-US/docs/JavaScript/Reference/Global_Objects/Math); for example:

```
var x = Math.floor(3.4890)
var ran = Math.round(Math.random()*100)
```

Browser Objects

Browser objects give us access to a browser and its properties like URLs; for example:

```
window.location.href = 'http://rapidprototypingwithjs.com'
console.log('test')
```

DOM Objects

DOM objects or DOM (https://developer.mozilla.org/en/docs/Web/API/Node) nodes are the browser interface to the DOM elements rendered on the page. They have properties such as width, height, position, and so on, and, of course, inner content, which can be another element or text. To get a DOM node, you can use its ID; for example:

```
var transactionsContainer = document.createElement('div')
transactionsContainer.setAttribute('id', 'main')
var content = document.createTextNode('Transactions')
transactionsContainer.appendChild(content)
document.body.appendChild(transactionsContainer)
var main = document.getElementById('main')
console.log(main, main.offsetWidth, main.offsetHeight)
```

Globals

In addition to classes such as String, Array, Number, and Math, which have a lot of useful methods, you can call the following methods known as globals, meaning you can invoke them from anywhere in your code:

- encodeURI (https://developer.mozilla.org/en-US/docs/Web/JavaScript/Reference/Global_Objects/encodeURI): Encodes a Uniform Resource Identifier (URI) to give you a URL; for example, encodeURI('http://www.webapplog.com/js is awesome')

- decodeURI (https://developer.mozilla.org/en-US/docs/Web/JavaScript/Reference/Global_Objects/decodeURI): Decodes a URI

- encodeURIComponent (https://developer.mozilla.org/en-US/docs/Web/JavaScript/Reference/Global_Objects/encodeURIComponent): Encode URI for URL parameters (don't use it for the entire URL string)

- decodeURIComponent (https://developer.mozilla.org/en-US/docs/Web/JavaScript/Reference/Global_Objects/decodeURIComponent): Decodes the fragment

- isNaN (https://developer.mozilla.org/en/docs/Web/JavaScript/Reference/Global_Objects/isNaN): Determines whether a value is a number or not

- JSON (https://developer.mozilla.org/en-US/docs/Web/JavaScript/Reference/Global_Objects/JSON): Parsing (parse()) and serializing (stringify()) of JSON data

11

- parseFloat (https://developer.mozilla.org/en/docs/Web/JavaScript/Reference/Global_Objects/parseFloat): Converts a string to a floating number

- parseInt (https://developer.mozilla.org/en-US/docs/Web/JavaScript/Reference/Global_Objects/parseInt): Converts a string to a number

- Intl (https://developer.mozilla.org/en-US/docs/Web/JavaScript/Reference/Global_Objects/Intl): Language-specific string comparison methods

- Error (https://developer.mozilla.org/en-US/docs/Web/JavaScript/Reference/Global_Objects/Error): An error object that you can use to instantiate your own error objects; for example, throw new Error('This book rocks!')

- Date (https://developer.mozilla.org/en-US/docs/Web/JavaScript/Reference/Global_Objects/Date): Various methods to work with dates

Conventions

JavaScript uses a number of style conventions. One of them is camelCase, in which you type multiple words as one word, capitalizing the first characters of the each word starting from the second one.

Semicolons are optional. Names starting with an underscore are private methods or attributes, but not because they are protected by the language. We use _ to simply to alert the developers not to use them because they might change in the future.

JavaScript supports numbers only up to 53 bits in size. Check out large numbers' libraries if you need to deal with numbers larger than that.

The full references for JavaScript and DOM objects are available at Mozilla Developer Network (https://developer.mozilla.org/en-US/docs/JavaScript/Reference) and w3school (http://www.w3schools.com/jsref/default.asp).

For JS resources such as ECMA specs, check out the list at JavaScript Language Resources (https://developer.mozilla.org/en-US/docs/JavaScript/Language_Resources). As of this writing, the latest JavaScript specification is ECMA-262 Edition 5.1 (http://www.ecma-international.org/publications/files/ECMA-ST/Ecma-262.pdf) and HTML (http://www.ecma-international.org/ecma-262/5.1/).

Another important distinction of JS is that it's a functional and prototypal language. Typical syntax for function declaration looks like this:

```
function Sum(a,b) {
  var sum = a + b
  return sum
}
console.log(Sum(1, 2))
```

Functions in JavaScript are first-class citizens (http://en.wikipedia.org/wiki/First-class_function) due to the functional programming (http://en.wikipedia.org/wiki/Functional_programming) nature of the language. Therefore, functions can be used as other variables or objects; for example, functions can be passed to other functions as arguments:

```
var f = function (str1){
  return function(str2){
  return str1 + ' ' + str2
  }
}
var a = f('hello')
var b = f('goodbye')
console.log((a('Catty')))
console.log((b('Doggy')))
```

It's good to know that there are several ways to instantiate an object in JS:

- Classical inheritance (http://www.crockford.com/javascript/inheritance.html) pattern

- Pseudo-classical inheritance (http://javascript.info/tutorial/pseudo-classical-pattern) pattern

- Functional inheritance pattern

For further reading on inheritance patterns, check out Inheritance Patterns in JavaScript (http://bolinfest.com/javascript/inheritance.php) and Inheritance revisited (https://developer.mozilla.org/en-US/docs/JavaScript/Guide/Inheritance_Revisited).

More information about browser-run JavaScript is available at Mozilla Developer Network (https://developer.mozilla.org/en-US/docs/JavaScript/Reference), Wikipedia (http://en.wikipedia.org/wiki/JavaScript), and w3schools (http://www.w3schools.com/js/default.asp).

Agile Methodologies

The Agile software development methodology evolved due to the fact that traditional methods like Waterfall weren't good enough in situations of high unpredictability; that is, when the solution is unknown (http://www.startuplessonslearned.com/2009/03/combining-agile-development-with.html). Agile methodology includes Scrum/sprint, test-driven development, continuous deployment, paired programming, and other practical techniques, many of which were borrowed from extreme programming.

Scrum

In regard to management, the Agile methodology uses the Scrum approach. More about Scrum can be read at the following sources:

- Scrum Guide in PDF (`http://www.scrumguides.org/docs/scrumguide/v1/scrum-guide-us.pdf`)

- Scrum.org (`http://www.scrum.org/`)

- Scrum development Wikipedia article (`http://en.wikipedia.org/wiki/Scrum_(development)`)

The Scrum methodology is a sequence of short cycles, and each cycle is called a *sprint*. One sprint usually lasts from one to two weeks. A typical sprint starts and ends with a sprint planning meeting where new tasks are assigned to team members. New tasks cannot be added to the sprint in progress; they can be added only at the sprint meetings.

An essential part of the Scrum methodology is the daily scrum meeting, hence the name. Each scrum is a 5- to 15-minute-long meeting, often conducted in a hallway. In scrum meetings, each team member answers three questions:

1. What have you done since yesterday?

2. What are you going to do today?

3. Do you need anything from other team members?

Flexibility makes Agile an improvement over the Waterfall methodology, especially in situations of high uncertainty (i.e., in startups).

The advantage of Scrum methodology is that it is effective where it is hard to plan ahead of time, and also in situations where a feedback loop is used as the main decision-making authority.

Test-Driven Development

Test-driven development (TDD) consists of the following steps:

1. Write failing automated test cases for new features, tasks, or enhancement by using assertions that are either true or false.

2. Write code to successfully pass the test cases.

3. Refactor code if needed, and add functionality while keeping the test cases passed.

4. Repeat until all tasks are complete.

Tests can be split into functional and unit testing. The latter is when a system tests individual units, methods, and functions with dependencies mocked up, whereas the former (also called integration testing) is when a system tests a slice of a functionality, including dependencies.

There are several advantages of TDD:

- Fewer bugs and defects

- More efficient codebase

- Confidence that code works and doesn't break the old functionality

Continuous Deployment and Integration

Continuous deployment (CD) is a set of techniques to rapidly deliver new features, bug fixes, and enhancements to the customers. CD includes automated testing and automated deployment. Using CD, manual overhead is decreased and feedback loop time is minimized. Basically, the faster a developer can get the feedback from the customers, the sooner the product can pivot, which leads to more advantages over the competition. Many startups deploy multiple times in a single day in comparison to the 6- to 12-month release cycle that is still typical for corporations and big companies.

The advantages of the CD approach include decreased feedback loop time and manual labor overhead.

The difference between CD and continuous integration is outlined in the post `Continuous Delivery vs. Continuous Deployment vs. Continuous Integration - Wait huh?` (`http://blog.assembla.com/assemblablog/tabid/12618/bid/92411/Continuous-Delivery-vs-Continuous-Deployment-vs-Continuous-Integration-Wait-huh.aspx`)

Some of the most popular solutions for continuous integration include the following:

- *Jenkins* (`http://jenkins-ci.org/`): An extendable open source continuous integration server

- *CircleCI* (`https://circleci.com/`): Ship better code, faster

- *Travis CI* (`https://travis-ci.org/`): A hosted continuous integration service for the open source community

Pair Programming

Pair programming is a technique when two developers work together in one environment. One of the developers is a driver, and the other is an observer. The driver writes code, and the observer assists by watching and making suggestions. Then they switch roles. The driver has a more tactical role of focusing on the current task. In contrast, the observer has a more strategic role, overseeing "the bigger picture" and finding bugs and ways to improve an algorithm.

The following are the advantages of paired programming:

- Pairs result in shorter and more efficient codebase, and introduce fewer bugs and defects.

- As an added bonus, knowledge is passed among programmers as they work together. However, conflicts between developers are possible, and not uncommon at all.

Back-End Definitions

The back end is another name for the server. It's everything after the browser. It includes server platforms like PHP, Python, Java, Ruby, and of course Node.js, as well as databases and other technologies.

Luckily, with modern back-end-as-a-service solutions you can bypass the back-end development entirely. With just a single <script> tag included, you can get a real-time database with the ability to put some logic into it like access level control (ALC), validation, and so on. I'm talking about Firebase.com and Parse.com.

In those cases where you still need your own custom server code, Node.js is the weapon of choice!

Node.js

Node.js is an open source, event-driven asynchronous I/O technology for building scalable and efficient web servers. Node.js consists of Google's V8 JavaScript engine (http://en.wikipedia.org/wiki/V8_(JavaScript_engine)). It was maintained by cloud company Joyent (http://joyent.com), but moved to the Technical Steering Committee governance.

The purpose and use of Node.js is similar to Twisted (http://twistedmatrix.com/trac/) for Python and EventMachine (http://rubyeventmachine.com/) for Ruby. The JavaScript implementation of Node was the third one after attempts at using Ruby and C++ programming languages.

Node.js is not in itself a framework like Ruby on Rails; it's more comparable to the pair of PHP and Apache. I'll provide a list of the top Node.js frameworks chapter 6.

The following are the advantages of using Node.js:

- Developers have high likelihood of familiarity with JavaScript due to its status as a de facto standard for web and mobile development

- Using one language for front-end and back-end development speeds up the coding process. A developer's brain doesn't have to switch between different syntaxes, a so-called context switch. The learning of methods and classes goes faster.

- With Node.js, you could prototype quickly and go to market to do your customer development and customer acquisition early. This is an important competitive advantage over other companies that use less agile technologies (e.g., PHP and MySQL).

- Node.js is built to support real-time applications by utilizing web sockets.

For more information go to Wikipedia (http://en.wikipedia.org/wiki/Nodejs), Nodejs.org (http://nodejs.org/about/), and articles on ReadWrite (http://readwrite.com/2011/01/25/wait-whats-nodejs-good-for-aga) and O'Reilly (http://radar.oreilly.com/2011/07/what-is-node.html).

For the current state of Node.js (as of this writing), refer to the official Node.js blog (https://nodejs.org/en/blog/).

NoSQL and MongoDB

MongoDB, from huMONGOus, is a high-performance, no-relationship database for huge quantities of data. The NoSQL concept came out when traditional relational database management systems (RDBMSs) were unable to meet the challenges of huge amounts of data.

Here are the advantages of using MongoDB:

- *Scalability:* Due to a distributed nature, multiple servers and data centers can have redundant data.

- *High performance:* MongoDB is very effective for storing and retrieving data, partially owing to the absence of relationships between elements and collections in the database.

- *Flexibility:* A key-value store is ideal for prototyping because it doesn't require developers to know the schema and there is no need for fixed data models or complex migrations.

Cloud Computing

Cloud computing consists of the following components:

- Infrastructure as a Service (IaaS), including Rackspace and Amazon Web Services

- Platform as a Service (PaaS), including Heroku and Windows Azure

- Back end as a Service (BaaS), the newest, coolest kid on the block, including Parse.com and Firebase

- Software as a Service (SaaS), including Google Apps and Salesforce.com

Cloud application platforms provide the following advantages:

- Scalability; for example, they can spawn new instances in a matter of minutes

- Ease of deployment; for example, to push to Heroku you can just use $ git push

- Pay-as-you-go plans where users add or remove memory and disk space based on demands

- Add-ons for easier installation and configuration of databases, app servers, packages, and so on

- Security and support

PaaS and BaaS are ideal for prototyping, building minimal viable products (MVP), and for early-stage startups in general.

Here is the list of the most popular PaaS solutions:

- Heroku (`http://heroku.com`)

- Windows Azure (`http://windowsazure.com`)

- Nodejitsu (`http://nodejitsu.com`)

- Nodester (`http://nodester.com`)

HTTP Requests and Responses

Each HTTP Request and Response consists of the following components:

- *Header*: Information about encoding, length of the body, origin, content type, and so on

- *Body*: Content, usually parameters or data, that is passed to the server or sent back to a client

In addition, the HTTP Request contains these elements:

- *Method*: There are several methods with the most common being `GET`, `POST`, `PUT`, and `DELETE`

- *URL*: Host, port, path; for example, `https://graph.facebook.com/498424660219540`

- *Query string*: Everything after a question mark in the URL (e.g., `?q=rpjs&page=20`)

RESTful API

RESTful (REpresentational State Transfer) API became popular due to the demand in distributed systems whereby each transaction needs to include enough information about the state of the client. In a sense, this standard is stateless because no information about the clients' states is stored on the server, thus making it possible for each request to be served by a different system.

Here are some of the distinct characteristics of RESTful API:

- It has better scalability support due to the fact that different components can be independently deployed to different servers.

- It replaced Simple Object Access Protocol (SOAP) because of the simpler verb and noun structure.

- It uses HTTP methods such as `GET`, `POST`, `DELETE`, `PUT`, `OPTIONS`, and so on.

Table 1-1 is an example of a simple Create, Read, Update and Delete (CRUD) RESTful API for Message Collection.

Table 1-1. *An Example of a CRUD RESTful API*

Method	URL	Meaning
GET	/messages.json	Return list of messages in JSON format
PUT	/messages.json	Update/replace all messages and return status/error in JSON
POST	/messages.json	Create new message and return its ID in JSON format
GET	/messages/{id}.json	Return message with ID {id} in JSON format
PUT	/messages/{id}.json	Update/replace message with ID {id}, if {id} message doesn't exist, create it
DELETE	/messages/{id}.json	Delete message with *id* {id}, return status/error in JSON format

REST is not a protocol; it is an architecture in the sense that it's more flexible than SOAP, which is a protocol. Therefore, REST API URLs could look like /messages/list.html or /messages/list.xml in case we want to support these formats.

PUT and DELETE are idempotent methods (http://en.wikipedia.org/wiki/Hypertext_Transfer_Protocol#Idempotent_methods_and_web_applications), which means that if the server receives two or more similar requests, the end result will be the same.

GET is nullipotent and POST is not idempotent and might affect state and cause side effects.

Further reading on REST API can be found at Wikipedia (http://en.wikipedia.org/wiki/Representational_state_transfer) and A Brief Introduction to REST article (http://www.infoq.com/articles/rest-introduction).

Summary

This concludes the first chapter. In this chapter we've covered some of the core concepts of web development. They'll be a solid foundation for the rest of the book. I'm sure some of the concepts were familiar to you:

- HTML

- CSS

- JavaScript types and objects

- Agile

- Node.js

- NoSQL

- HTTP Request

- RESTful API

Nevertheless, it's good to brush up on them because they are numerous and vast. Theory is not that useful or interesting without understanding how it applies and benefits the actual code. Therefore, we'll move swiftly to the technical setup to get you to the coding projects fast.

CHAPTER 2

Setup

One of my most productive days was throwing away 1,000 lines of code.

—Ken Thompson

In this chapter, we1 cover the following topics:

- Suggestions for the toolset
- Step-by-step installation of local components
- Preparation for the use of cloud services

The proper setup is absolutely crucial to the productive development. You need to have everything ready when you embark on a long journey, right? The toolset will make you productive, and the other installations are dependencies like Node.js or MongoDB. They enable the server-side code and persistence, respectively. In addition to that, in the cloud section, we cover setup of the services for deployment and development. They will enable you to keep your code under version control and deploy in a scalable manner.

Local Setup

Local setup is what we use on our development machines when we work on the project. It includes anything from folders, browsers, editors, and HTTP servers to databases. Figure 2-1 shows an example of the initial development environment setup.

```
● ● ●                      fullstack-javascript — bash
Azats-Air:~ azat$ cd ~/Documents
Azats-Air:Documents azat$ mkdir Development
Azats-Air:Documents azat$ cd Development/
Azats-Air:Development azat$ mkdir fullstack-javascript
Azats-Air:Development azat$ cd fullstack-javascript/
Azats-Air:fullstack-javascript azat$
```

Figure 2-1. *Initial development environment setup*

Development Folder

If you don't have a specific development folder for your web development projects, you could create a Development folder in the Documents folder (path will be Documents/ Development). To work on the code example, create a fullstack-javascript folder inside your web development projects folder; for example, if you create a fullstack-javascript folder inside of the Development folder, the path will be Documents/ Development/fullstack-javascript. You could use the Finder on Mac OS X or the following terminal commands on OS X/Linux systems:

```
$ cd ~/Documents
$ mkdir Development
$ cd Development
$ mkdir fullstack-javascript
```

■ **Tip**   To open Mac OS Finder app in the current directory from Terminal, just type and run the $ open . command. On Windows, Terminal is command prompt.

To get the list of files and folders, use this UNIX/Linux command:

```
$ ls
```

or to display hidden files and folders, like .git, use this:

```
$ ls -lah
```

Another alternative to $ ls is $ ls -alt. The difference between the -lah and the -alt options is that the latter sorts items chronologically and the former sorts them alphabetically.

You can use the Tab key to autocomplete names of the files and folders.

Later, you could copy examples into the fullstack-javascript folder as well as create apps in that folder.

■ **Tip**   Another useful thing is to have the New Terminal at Folder option in Finder on Mac OS X. To enable it, open your System Preferences (you could use Command + Space, a.k.a. Spotlight, for it). Find Keyboard and click it. Open Keyboard Shortcuts and click Services. Select the New Terminal at Folder and New Terminal Tab at Folder check boxes. Close the window (optional).

Browsers

We recommend downloading the latest version of the WebKit (http://en.wikipedia.org/wiki/WebKit) or Gecko at http://en.wikipedia.org/wiki/Gecko_(layout_engine) browser of your choice:

- Chrome (http://www.google.com/chrome) (recommended)
- Safari (http://www.apple.com/safari/)
- Firefox (http://www.mozilla.org/en-US/firefox/new)

Whereas Chrome and Safari already come with built-in developer tools, you'll need the Firebug plug-in for Firefox (Figure 2-2).

Figure 2-2. *Chrome Developer Tools in action*

Firebug and developer tools allow developers to do many things, including these:

- Debug JavaScript
- Manipulate HTML and DOM elements
- Modify CSS on the fly
- Monitor HTTP requests and responses
- Run profiles and inspect heap dumps
- See loaded assets such as images, CSS, and JS files

There are some great Chrome Developer Tools (DevTools) tutorials, such as the following and those shown in Figures 2-3 and 2-4:

- Explore and Master Chrome DevTools (`http://discover-devtools.codeschool.com/`) with Code School

- Chrome DevTools videos (`https://developers.google.com/chrome-developer-tools/docs/videos`)

- Chrome DevTools overview (`https://developers.google.com/chrome-developer-tools`)

Figure 2-3. *Google tutorials for mastering web developer tools*

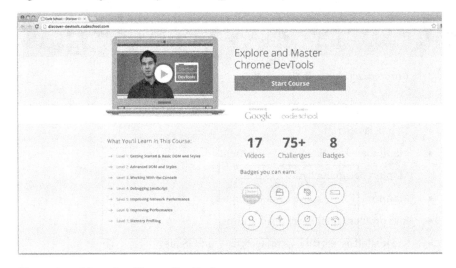

Figure 2-4. *Mastering Chrome DevTools*

IDEs and Text Editors

One of the best things about JavaScript is that you don't need to compile the code. Because JS lives in and is run in a browser, you can do debugging right there, in a browser! It's an interpreted language, not a compiled one. Therefore, we highly recommend a lightweight text editor instead of a full-blown integrated development environment (http://en.wikipedia.org/wiki/Integrated_development_environment), or IDE, but if you are already familiar and comfortable with the IDE of your choice like Eclipse, (http://www.eclipse.org/) NetBeans (http://netbeans.org/) or Aptana (http://aptana.com/), feel free to stick with it.

Here is the list of the most popular text editors and IDEs used in web development:

- *TextMate* (http://macromates.com/): Mac OS X version only, free 30-day trial for v1.5, dubbed The Missing Editor for Mac OS X.

- *Sublime Text* (http://www.sublimetext.com/): Mac OS X and Windows versions are available. This is an even better alternative to TextMate, with an unlimited evaluation period (Figure 2-5).

Figure 2-5. *Sublime Text code editor home page*

- *Coda* (http://panic.com/coda/): All-in-one editor with FTP browser and preview, has support for development with and on an iPad.

- Aptana Studio (http://aptana.com/): Full-sized IDE with a built-in terminal and many other tools.

- *Notepad* ++ (http:notepad-plus-plus.org/): Free Windows-only lightweight text editor with the support of many languages.

- *WebStorm IDE* (`http://www.jetbrains.com/webstorm/`):
  Feature-rich IDE that allows for Node.js debugging. It is
  developed by JetBrains and marketed as the smartest JavaScript
  IDE (Figure 2-6).

Figure 2-6. *WebStorm IDE home page*

- *MS Visual Studio* (`https://www.visualstudio.com/features/`
  `node-js-vs`): Node.js tools for the famous Visual Studio
  environment from a small Redmond company.

Version Control Systems

A version control system (`http://en.wikipedia.org/wiki/Revision_control`) is a
must-have even in an only-one-developer situation. Also many cloud services (e.g.,
Heroku) require Git for deployment. We also highly recommend getting used to Git and
Git terminal commands instead of using Git visual clients and apps with a GUI: GitX
(`http://gitx.frim.nl/`), Gitbox (`http://www.gitboxapp.com/`) or GitHub for Mac
(`http://mac.github.com/`).

Subversion is a nondistributed version control system. This article compares
Git vs. Subversion (`https://git.wiki.kernel.org/index.php/GitSvnComparison`).

Here are the steps to install and set up Git on your machine:

1. Download the latest version for your OS at `http://git-scm.com/downloads` (Figure 2-7).

Figure 2-7. *Downloading latest release of Git*

2. Install Git from the downloaded `*.dmg` package; that is, run the `*.pkg` file and follow the wizard.

3. Find the terminal app by using Command + Space, a.k.a. Spotlight (Figure 2-8), on OS X. For Windows you could use PuTTY (`http://www.chiark.greenend.org.uk/~sgtatham/putty/`) or Cygwin (`http://www.cygwin.com/`).

27

Figure 2-8. *Using Spotlight to find and run an application*

4. In your terminal, type these commands, substituting `"John Doe"` and johndoe@example.com with your name and e-mail:

```
$ git config --global user.name "John Doe"
$ git config --global user.email johndoe@example.com
```

5. To check the installation, run command:

```
$ git version
```

6. You should see something like this in your terminal window (your version might vary; in our case it's 1.8.3.2, as shown in Figure 2-9):

```
git version 1.8.3.2
```

Figure 2-9. *Configuring and testing Git installation*

Generating SSH keys and uploading them to SaaS/PaaS web sites will be covered later.

Local HTTP Servers

Although you can do most of the front-end development without a local HTTP server, it is needed for loading files with HTTP Requests/AJAX calls. Also, it's just good practice in general to use a local HTTP server. This way, your development environment is as close to the production environment as possible.

I recommend you use Node-based tools as static web servers. They lack GUIs, but they are simple and fast. You can install them with npm (comes with Node.js; instructions are later in this chapter):

- *node-static* (https://github.com/cloudhead/node-static):
  Static file server with built-in caching.

- *http-server* (https://www.npmjs.com/package/http-server):
  Zero-configuration command-line HTTP server.

If you prefer something with GUIs to a command-line interface (CLI), you might want to consider the following modifications of the Apache web server. MAMP, MAMP Stack, and XAMPP have intuitive GUIs that allow you to change configurations and host file settings.

- *MAMP* (http://www.mamp.info/en/index.html): Mac, Apache, MySQL, PHP personal web server for Mac OS X.

- *MAMP Stack* (http://bitnami.com/stack/mamp): Mac app with PHP, Apache, MySQL, and phpMyAdmin stack build by BitNami (Apple App Store) (https://itunes.apple.com/es/app/mamp-stack/id571310406?l=en).

- *XAMPP* (http://www.apachefriends.org/en/xampp.html): Apache distribution containing MySQL, PHP and Perl for Windows, Mac, Linux, and Solaris.

The MAMP for Mac home page is shown in Figure 2-10.

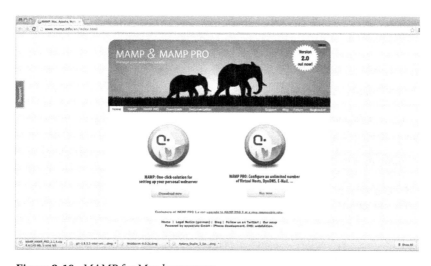

Figure 2-10. *MAMP for Mac home page*

Database: MongoDB

The following steps are better suited for Mac OS X/Linux-based systems, but with some modification they can be used for Windows systems as well (i.e., $PATH variable, Step 3). Here we describe the MongoDB installation from the official package, because we found that this approach is more robust and leads to less conflicts. However, there are many other ways to install it on Mac (http://docs.mongodb.org/manual/tutorial/install-mongodb-on-os-x/), for example using Brew, as well as on other systems (http://docs.mongodb.org/manual/installation/).

1. MongoDB can be downloaded at (http://www.mongodb.org/downloads). For the latest Apple laptops, like MacBook Air, select OS X 64-bit version. The owners of older Macs should browse the link at (http://dl.mongodb.org/dl/osx/i386).

■ **Tip** To figure out the architecture type of your processor, type the $ `uname -p` at the command line.

---

2. Unpack the package into your web development folder (~/Documents/Development or any other). If you want, you could install MongoDB into the /usr/local/mongodb folder.

3. Optional: If you would like to access MongoDB commands from anywhere on your system, you need to add your mongodb path to the $PATH variable. For Mac OS X the open system *paths* file with:

    sudo vi /etc/paths

    or, if you prefer TextMate:

    mate /etc/paths

    And add this line to the /etc/paths file:

    /usr/local/mongodb/bin

4. Create a data folder; by default, MongoDB uses /data/db. Please note that this might be different in new versions of MongoDB. To create it, type and execute the following commands in the terminal (Figure 2-11):

    ```
    $ sudo mkdir -p /data/db
    $ sudo chown `id -u` /data/db
    ```

```
● ○ ○                    Terminal — bash — 79×6
Last login: Sun Aug 25 17:28:35 on ttys000
Azats-Air:~ azat$ sudo mkdir /data/db
Azats-Air:~ azat$ sudo chown `id -u` /data/db
Azats-Air:~ azat$ ▎
```

Figure 2-11. *Initial setup for MongoDB: Create the data directory*

If you prefer to use a path other than /data/db you could specify it using the --dbpath option to mongod (the main MongoDB service).

5. Go to the folder where you unpacked MongoDB. That location should have a bin folder in it. From there, type the following command in your terminal:

    $ ./bin/mongod

6. If you see something like the following (and as in Figure 2-12) it means that the MongoDB database server is running:

    MongoDB starting: pid =7218 port=27017...

    By default, it's listening at http://localhost:27017. If you go to your browser and type http://localhost:28017 you should be able to see the version number, logs, and other useful information. In this case the MondoDB server is using two different ports (27017 and 28017): One is primary (native) for the communications with apps and the other is a web-based GUI for monitoring and statistics. In our Node.js code we'll be using only 27017. Don't forget to restart the Terminal window after adding a new path to the $PATH variable.

    Now, to take it even further, we can test to determine if we have access to the MongoDB console/shell, which will act as a client to this server. This means that we'll have to keep the terminal window with the server open and running.

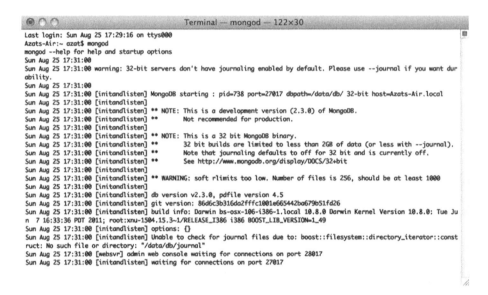

```
Last login: Sun Aug 25 17:29:16 on ttys000
Azats-Air:~ azat$ mongod
mongod --help for help and startup options
Sun Aug 25 17:31:00
Sun Aug 25 17:31:00 warning: 32-bit servers don't have journaling enabled by default. Please use --journal if you want dur
ability.
Sun Aug 25 17:31:00
Sun Aug 25 17:31:00 [initandlisten] MongoDB starting : pid=738 port=27017 dbpath=/data/db/ 32-bit host=Azats-Air.local
Sun Aug 25 17:31:00 [initandlisten]
Sun Aug 25 17:31:00 [initandlisten] ** NOTE: This is a development version (2.3.0) of MongoDB.
Sun Aug 25 17:31:00 [initandlisten] **          Not recommended for production.
Sun Aug 25 17:31:00 [initandlisten]
Sun Aug 25 17:31:00 [initandlisten] ** NOTE: This is a 32 bit MongoDB binary.
Sun Aug 25 17:31:00 [initandlisten] **          32 bit builds are limited to less than 2GB of data (or less with --journal).
Sun Aug 25 17:31:00 [initandlisten] **          Note that journaling defaults to off for 32 bit and is currently off.
Sun Aug 25 17:31:00 [initandlisten] **          See http://www.mongodb.org/display/DOCS/32+bit
Sun Aug 25 17:31:00 [initandlisten]
Sun Aug 25 17:31:00 [initandlisten] ** WARNING: soft rlimits too low. Number of files is 256, should be at least 1000
Sun Aug 25 17:31:00 [initandlisten]
Sun Aug 25 17:31:00 [initandlisten] db version v2.3.0, pdfile version 4.5
Sun Aug 25 17:31:00 [initandlisten] git version: 86d6c3b316da2fffc1001e665442ba679b51fd26
Sun Aug 25 17:31:00 [initandlisten] build info: Darwin bs-osx-106-i386-1.local 10.8.0 Darwin Kernel Version 10.8.0: Tue Ju
n  7 16:33:36 PDT 2011; root:xnu-1504.15.3~1/RELEASE_I386 i386 BOOST_LIB_VERSION=1_49
Sun Aug 25 17:31:00 [initandlisten] options: {}
Sun Aug 25 17:31:00 [initandlisten] Unable to check for journal files due to: boost::filesystem::directory_iterator::const
ruct: No such file or directory: "/data/db/journal"
Sun Aug 25 17:31:00 [websvr] admin web console waiting for connections on port 28017
Sun Aug 25 17:31:00 [initandlisten] waiting for connections on port 27017
```

Figure 2-12. *Starting up the MongoDB server*

7. Open another terminal window at the same folder and execute:

```
$ ./bin/mongo
```

You should be able to see something like "MongoDB shell version 2.0.6 ..."

8. Then type and execute:

```
> db.test.save( { a: 1 } )
> db.test.find()
```

If you see that your record is being saved, then everything went well (Figure 2-13).

```
●●○            Terminal — mongo — 79×14
Last login: Sun Aug 25 17:30:33 on ttys000
Azats-Air:~ azat$ mongo
MongoDB shell version: 2.3.0
connecting to: test
Welcome to the MongoDB shell.
For interactive help, type "help".
For more comprehensive documentation, see
        http://docs.mongodb.org/
Questions? Try the support group
        http://groups.google.com/group/mongodb-user
> db.test.save( { a: 1} )
> db.test.find()
{ "_id" : ObjectId("521a169d6421d0d4d6f3190f"), "a" : 1 }
>
```

Figure 2-13. *Running MongoDB client and storing sample data*

Commands find and save do exactly what you might think they do.

Detailed instructions are also available at MongoDB.org: Install MongoDB on OS X (http://docs.mongodb.org/manual/tutorial/install-mongodb-on-os-x). For Windows users there is a good walk-through article at Installing MongoDB (http://www.tuanleaded.com/blog/2011/10/installing-mongodb).

■ **Note**   MAMP and XAMPP applications come with MySQL—an open source traditional SQL database—and phpMyAdmin—a web interface for MySQL database.

On Mac OS X (and most UNIX systems), to close the process use Control + C. If you use Control + Z it will put the process to sleep (or detach the terminal window); in this case, you might end up with the lock on data files and will have to use the kill command or Activity Monitor, and manually delete the locked file in the data folder. In vanilla Mac Terminal Command + . is an alternative to Control + C.

Other Components

These are required technologies. Please make sure you have them before proceeding to the next chapter.

1. *Node.js*: We need it for build tools and back-end apps.

2. *Browser JS libraries*: We need them for front-end apps.

3. *LESS app*: We need it to compile LESS into CSS (Mac OS X only).

Node.js Installation

Node.js is available at `http://nodejs.org/#download` (Figure 2-14). The installation is trivial: Download the archive and run the `*.pkg` package installer. To check the installation of Node.js, you could type and execute:

```
$ node -v
```

Figure 2-14. *Node.js home page*

I use v5.1.0 for this book and tested all examples with v5.1.0. If you use another version, do so at your own risk. I cannot guarantee that the examples will run.
Assuming you have 5.1.0, it should show something similar to this:

```
v5.1.0
```

If you want to switch between multiple versions of Node.js, there are solutions for that:

- *nvm* (`https://github.com/creationix/nvm`): Node.js Version Manager

- *Nave* (`https://github.com/isaacs/nave`): Virtual environments for Node.js

- *n* (`https://github.com/tj/n`): Node.js version management

The Node.js package already includes Node Package Manager (`https://npmjs.org`) (NPM). We'll use NPM extensively to install Node.js modules.

Browser JavaScript Libraries

Front-end JavaScript libraries are downloaded and unpacked from their respective web sites. Those files are usually put in the Development folder (e.g., ~/Documents/Development) for future use. Often, there is a choice between the minified production version (more on that in the AMD and Require.js section of Chapter 4) and the extensively rich in comments development one.

Another approach is to hot-link these scripts from CDNs such as Google Hosted Libraries (https://developers.google.com/speed/libraries/devguide), CDNJS (http://cdnjs.com/), Microsoft Ajax Content Delivery Network (http://www.asp.net/ajaxlibrary/cdn.ashx), and others. By doing so the apps will be faster for some users, but won't work locally at all without the Internet.

- LESS as a front-end interpreter is available at lesscss.org. You could unpack it into your development folder (~/Documents/Development) or any other folder.

- Twitter Bootstrap is a CSS/LESS framework. It's available at twitter.github.com/bootstrap.

- jQuery is available at jquery.com.

- Backbone.js is available at backbonejs.org.

- Underscore.js is available at underscorejs.org.

- Require.js is available at requirejs.org.

LESS App

The LESS App is a Mac OS X application for "on-the-fly" compilation of LESS to CSS. It's available at incident57.com/less (Figure 2-15).

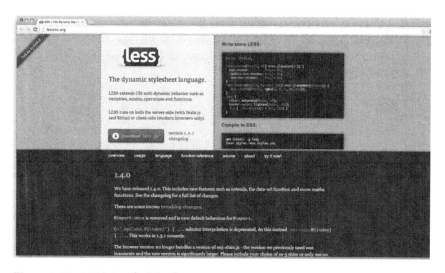

Figure 2-15. *LESS App for Mac home page*

Cloud Setup

The Cloud setup discussed in the following sections will allow you to keep your code under version control and deploy in a scalable manner.

SSH Keys

SSH keys provide a secure connection without the need to enter user name and password every time. For GitHub repositories, the latter approach is used with HTTPS URLs; for example, `https://github.com/azat-co/fullstack-javascript.git`; and the former with SSH URLs; for example, `git@github.com:azat-co/fullstack-javascript.git`.

To generate SSH keys for GitHub on Mac OS X/UNIX machines do the following:

1. Check for existing SSH keys:

   ```
   $ cd ~/.ssh
   $ ls -lah
   ```

2. If you see some files like `id_rsa` (please refer to Figure 2-16 for an example), you could delete them or back them up into a separate folder by using the following commands:

   ```
   $ mkdir key_backup
   $ cp id_rsa* key_backup
   $ rm id_rsa*
   ```

3. Now we can generate a new SSH key pair using the `ssh-keygen` command, assuming we are in the `~/.ssh` folder:

   ```
   $ ssh-keygen -t rsa -C "your_email@youremail.com"
   ```

4. Answer the questions; it is better to keep the default name of `id_rsa`. Then copy the content of the `id_rsa.pub` file to your clipboard (Figure 2-16):

   ```
   $ pbcopy < ~/.ssh/id_rsa.pub
   ```

```
Azats-Air:~ azat$ ssh-keygen -t rsa -C "johny@example.com"
Generating public/private rsa key pair.
Enter file in which to save the key (/Users/azat/.ssh/id_rsa):
Created directory '/Users/azat/.ssh'.
Enter passphrase (empty for no passphrase):
Enter same passphrase again:
Your identification has been saved in /Users/azat/.ssh/id_rsa.
Your public key has been saved in /Users/azat/.ssh/id_rsa.pub.
The key fingerprint is:
df:08:f9:a0:0c:87:ed:e8:38:33:92:11:54:c3:bb:0f johny@example.com
The key's randomart image is:
+--[ RSA 2048]----+
|  oo             |
| . ..            |
|.   .            |
|.  . o  .        |
| .  + o S        |
|.  E * . = o     |
| o + +   + .     |
|o +o .           |
| ..+.            |
+-----------------+
Azats-Air:~ azat$ open id_rsa.pub
The file /Users/azat/id_rsa.pub does not exist.
Azats-Air:~ azat$ open ~/.ssh/id_rsa.pub
No application knows how to open /Users/azat/.ssh/id_rsa.pub.
Azats-Air:~ azat$ pbcopy < ~/.ssh/id_rsa.pub
Azats-Air:~ azat$
```

Figure 2-16. *Generating RSA key for SSH and copying public key to clipboard*

5. Alternatively, open id_rsa.pub file in the default editor:

   ```
   $ open id_rsa.pub
   ```

6. Or in TextMate:

   ```
   $ mate id_rsa.pub
   ```

GitHub

1. After you have copied the public key, go to github.com, log in, go to your account settings, select SSH Key, and add the new SSH key. Assign a name, such as the name of your computer, and paste the value of your public key.

2. To check if you have an SSH connection to GitHub, type and execute the following command in your terminal:

   ```
   $ ssh -T git@github.com
   ```

   If you see something like this:

   ```
   Hi your-GitHub-username! You've successfully authenticated,
   but GitHub does not provide shell access.
   ```

   then everything is set up.

3. The first time you connect to GitHub, you can receive an Authenticity of Host ... Can't Be Established warning. Please don't be confused with such a message—just proceed by answering Yes as shown in Figure 2-17.

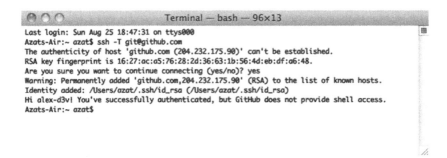

Figure 2-17. *Testing SSH connection to GitHub for the very first time*

If for some reason you have a different message, please repeat Steps 3 and 4 from the previous section on SSH keys or reupload the content of your *.pub file to GitHub.

■ **Warning**   Keep your id_rsa file private and don't share it with anybody!

More instructions are available at GitHub: Generating SSH Keys (https://help.github.com/articles/generating-ssh-keys).

Windows users might find the SSH key generator feature in [PuTTY] useful.

Windows Azure

Here are the steps to set up a Windows Azure account:

1. You'll need to sign up for Windows Azure Web Site and Virtual Machine previews. Currently they have a 90-day free trial available at https://azure.microsoft.com/en-us/.

2. Enable Git Deployment and create a user name and password, then upload the SSH public key to Windows Azure.

3. Install the Node.js SDK, which is available at https://azure.microsoft.com/en-us/develop/nodejs/.

4. To check your installation type:

    ```
    $ azure -v
    ```

    You should be able to see something like this:

    ```
    Windows Azure: Microsoft's Cloud Platform... Tool Version 0.6.0
    ```

5. Log in to Windows Azure Portal at `https://windows.azure.com/` (Figure 2-18).

Figure 2-18. *Registering on Windows Azure*

6. Select New, then select Web Site, and Quick Create. Type the name that will serve as the URL for your web site, and click OK.

7. Go to this newly created web site's Dashboard and select Set Up Git Publishing. Come up with a user name and password. This combination can be used to deploy to any web site in your subscription, meaning that you do not need to set credentials for every web site you create. Click OK.

8. On the follow-up screen, it should show you the Git URL to push to, something like this:

    `https://azatazure@azat.scm.azurewebsites.net/azat.git`

    You will also see instructions on how to proceed with deployment. We'll cover them later.

9. Advanced user option: Follow this tutorial to create a virtual machine and install MongoDB on it: `Install MongoDB on a virtual machine running CentOS Linux in Windows Azure` (`https://www.windowsazure.com/en-us/manage/linux/common-tasks/mongodb-on-a-linux-vm/`).

Heroku

Heroku is a polyglot agile application deployment platform (see `http://www.heroku.com/`). Heroku works similarly to Windows Azure in the sense that you can use Git to deploy applications. There is no need to install Virtual Machine for MongoDB because Heroku has a MongoHQ add-on (`https://addons.heroku.com/mongohq`).

To set up Heroku, follow these steps:

1. Sign up at (`http://heroku.com`). Currently they have a free account; to use it, select all options as minimum (0) and database as shared.

2. Download Heroku Toolbelt at (`https://toolbelt.heroku.com`). Toolbelt is a package of tools; that is, libraries that consist of Heroku, Git, and Foreman (`https://github.com/ddollar/foreman`). For users of older Macs, get this client (`https://github.com/heroku/heroku`) directly. If you utilize another OS, browse Heroku Client GitHub (`https://github.com/heroku/heroku`).

3. After the installation is done, you should have access to the heroku command. To check it and log in to Heroku, type:

    `$ heroku login`

    It will ask you for Heroku credentials (user name and password), and if you've already created the SSH key, it will automatically upload it to the Heroku web site (Figure 2-19).

```
● ○ ○                    Terminal — bash — 86×14
Last login: Sun Aug 25 21:04:33 on ttys000
Azats-Air:~ azat$ cd ~/Downloads/heroku-client/bin
Azats-Air:bin azat$ ./heroku login
Enter your Heroku credentials.
Email: alex.m4il.box@gmail.com
Password (typing will be hidden):
Authentication successful.
Azats-Air:bin azat$
```

Figure 2-19. *The response to the successful* `$ heroku login` *command*

4. If everything went well, to create a Heroku application inside of your specific project folder, you should be able to run this command:

    `$ heroku create`

    More detailed step-by-step instructions are available at Heroku: Quickstart (`https://devcenter.heroku.com/articles/quickstart`) and Heroku: Node.js (`https://devcenter.heroku.com/articles/nodejs`).

Summary

In this chapter, we've covered the technical setup of the version control system, cloud clients as well as installed various tools and libraries. We'll use these libraries and tools in the books, for this reason it's important to have them installed and ready to go. In addition, the chapter provided a few links to external resources which can make you understand and learn web development tools better. One of the most useful of such resources is DevTools.

You must be dying to get started with the actual coding. The wait is over. Meet the first fullstack JavaScript code in the next chapter.

CHAPTER 3

jQuery and Parse.com

There are two ways of constructing a software design: One way is to make it so simple that there are obviously no deficiencies, and the other way is to make it so complicated that there are no obvious deficiencies. The first method is far more difficult.

—Tony Hoare

This chapter covers the following topics:

- Definitions of JSON, AJAX, and CORS

- Overview of main jQuery functions

- Twitter Bootstrap scaffolding

- Main LESS components

- Illustrations of JSONP calls on OpenWeatherMap API example

- Parse.com overview

- Explanations on how to build a Message Board front-end only application with jQuery and Parse.com

- Step-by-step instructions on deployment to Windows Azure and Heroku

- Updating and deleting of messages

This chapter is a basic introduction to front-end web development. It covers things important to front-end development of apps such as Twitter Bootstrap and LESS. These amazing libraries allow developers to have a nice user interface in no time.

It covers the terminology and explains JSON, AJAX, and CORS. We then explore the example of a weather app.

We use Parse.com as our back end to streamline things and make development faster while still keeping it realistic. The cornerstone of this chapter is a persistent message board application built with Parse.com and jQuery.

Definitions

Before anything else, let's clarify some terms. They are important enough for us to pause and get familiar with them. If these are familiar to you, you might want to skip ahead.

JavaScript Object Notation

Here is the definition of JavaScript Object Notation (JSON) from `www.json.org`

JavaScript Object Notation, or JSON, is a lightweight data-interchange format. It is easy for humans to read and write. It is easy for machines to parse and generate. It is based on a subset of the JavaScript Programming Language, Standard ECMA-262 3rd Edition - December 1999 (`www.ecma-international.org/publications/files/ECMA-ST/Ecma-262.pdf`).

JSON is a text format that is completely language independent but uses conventions that are familiar to programmers of the C-family of languages, including C, C++, C#, Java, JavaScript, Perl, Python, and many others. These properties make JSON an ideal data-interchange language.

JSON has become a standard for transferring data between different components of web and mobile applications and third-party services. JSON is also widely used inside the applications as a format for configuration, locales, translation files, or any other data.

A typical JSON object looks like this:

```
{
  "a": "value of a",
  "b": "value of b"
}
```

We have an object with key/value pairs. Keys are on the left and values are on the right side of colons (:). In computer science terminology, JSON is equivalent to a hash table, a keyed list, or an associative array (depending on the particular language). The only big difference between JSON and JS object literal notation (native JS objects) is that the former is more stringent and requires double quotes (") for key identifiers and string values. Both types can be serialized into a string representation with `JSON.stringify()` and deserialized with `JSON.parse()`, assuming we have a valid JSON object in a string format.

However, every member of an object can be an array, primitive, or another object; for example:

```
{
  "posts": [{
    "title": "Get your mind in shape!",
    "votes": 9,
    "comments": ["nice!", "good link"]
  }, {
    "title": "Yet another post",
    "votes": 0,
    "comments": []
  }
  ],
```

```
  "totalPost": 2,
  "getData": function () {
    return new Data().getDate();
  }
}
```

In this example, we have an object with the posts property. The value of the posts property is an array of objects with each one of them having title, votes, and comments keys. The votes property holds a number primitive, whereas comments is an array of strings. We also can have functions as values; in this case, the key is called a method; that is, getData.

JSON is much more flexible and compact than XML or other data formats, as outlined in this article: JSON: The Fat-Free Alternative to XML (www.json.org/xml.html). Conveniently, MongoDB uses a JSON-like format called Binary JSON (http://bsonspec.org) (BSON), discussed further in BSON later in Chapter 7.

AJAX

Asynchronous JavaScript and XML (AJAX) is used on the client side (browser) to send and receive data from the server by utilizing an XMLHttpRequest object in JavaScript language. Despite the name, the use of XML is not required, and JSON is often used instead. That's why developers almost never say AJAX anymore. Keep in mind that HTTP requests could be made synchronously, but it's not a good practice to do so. The most typical example of a sync request would be the <script> tag inclusion.

Cross-Domain Calls

For security reasons, the initial implementation of an XMLHTTPRequest object did not allow for cross-domain calls, when a client-side code and a server-side one are on different domains. There are methods to work around this issue.

One of them is to use JSONP (http://en.wikipedia.org/wiki/JSONP), JSON with padding/prefix. It's basically a dynamic manipulation via DOM generated <script> tag. Script tags don't fall into the same domain limitation. The JSONP request includes the name of a callback function in a request query string. For example, the jQuery.ajax() function automatically generates a unique function name and appends it to the request (which is one string broken into multiple lines for readability):

```
https://graph.facebook.com/search
  ?type=post
  &limit=20
  &q=Gatsby
  &callback=jQuery16207184716751798987_1368412972614&_=1368412984735
```

The second approach is to use cross-origin resource sharing (CORS (http://www.w3.org/TR/cors)), which is a better solution, but it requires control over the server side to modify response headers. We use this technique in the final version of the Message Board example application. Here is an example of a CORS server response header:

```
Access-Control-Allow-Origin: *
```

More about CORS is available at Resources by Enable CORS (http://enable-cors.org/resources.html) and Using CORS by HTML5 Rocks Tutorials (http://www.html5rocks.com/en/tutorials/cors/). You can test CORS requests at test-cors.org.

jQuery Functions

During the training we'll be using jQuery (http://jquery.com/) for DOM manipulations, HTTP Requests, and JSONP calls. jQuery became a de facto standard because of its $ object or function, which provides a simple yet efficient way to access any HTML DOM element on a page by its ID, class, tag name, attribute value, structure, or any combination thereof. The syntax is very similar to CSS, where we use # for id and . for class selection. For example:

```
$('#main').hide()
$('p.large').attr('style','color:red')
$('#main').show().html('<div>new div</div>')
```

Here is the list of most commonly used jQuery API functions:

- find() (http://api.jquery.com/find): Selects elements based on the provided selector string

- hide() (http://api.jquery.com/hide): Hides an element if it was visible

- show() (http://api.jquery.com/show): Shows an element if it was hidden

- html() (http://api.jquery.com/html): Gets or sets an inner HTML of an element

- append() (http://api.jquery.com/append) Injects an element into the DOM after the selected element

- prepend() (http://api.jquery.com/prepend) Injects an element into the DOM before the selected element

- on() (http://api.jquery.com/on): Attaches an event listener to an element

- off() (http://api.jquery.com/off) Detaches an event listener from an element

- `css()` (http://api.jquery.com/css): Gets or sets the style attribute value of an element

- `attr()` (http://api.jquery.com/attr) Gets or sets any attribute of an element

- `val()` (http://api.jquery.com/val): Gets or sets the value attribute of an element

- `text()` (http://api.jquery.com/text): Gets the combined text of an element and its children

- `each()` (http://api.jquery.com/each): Iterates over a set of matched elements

Most jQuery functions act not only on a single element, on which they are called, but on a set of matched elements if the result of the selection has multiple items. This is a common pitfall that leads to bugs, and it usually happens when a jQuery selector is too broad.

Also, jQuery has many available plug-ins and libraries that provide a rich user interface or other functionality. For example:

- jQuery UI (http://jqueryui.com/)

- jQuery Mobile (http://jquerymobile.com/)

Twitter Bootstrap

Supplemental video which walks you through the implementation and demonstrates the project: http://bit.ly/1RKx9uY.

Twitter Bootstrap (http://getbootstrap.com) is a collection of CSS/LESS rules and JavaScript plug-ins for creating a good user interface and user experience without spending a lot of time on such details as rounded-edge buttons, cross-compatibility, responsiveness, and so on. This collection or framework is perfect for rapid prototyping of your ideas. Nevertheless, due to its ability to be customized, Twitter Bootstrap is also a good foundation for serious projects. The source code is written in LESS (http://lesscss.org), but plain CSS can be downloaded and used as well.

Here is a simple example of using Twitter Bootstrap scaffolding for the version v4.0.0-alpha. The structure of the project should look like this:

```
/01-bootstrap
  -index.html
  /css
    -bootstrap.css
    -bootstrap.min.css
    ... (other files if needed)
  /js
    -bootstrap.js
    -bootstrap.min.js
    -npm.js
```

First let's create the index.html file with proper tags:

```
<!DOCTYPE html>
<html lang="en">
  <head>

  </head>
  <body>
  </body>
</html>
```

Include the Twitter Bootstrap library as a minified CSS file:

```
<!DOCTYPE html>
<html lang="en">
  <head>
    <link
      type="text/css"
      rel="stylesheet"
      href="css/bootstrap.min.css" />
  </head>
  <body>
  </body>
</html>
```

Apply scaffolding with container-fluid and row-fluid classes:

```
<body >
  <div class="container-fluid">
    <div class="row-fluid">
    </div>  <!-- row-fluid -->
  </div>  <!-- container-fluid -->
</body>
```

Twitter Bootstrap uses a 12-column grid. The size of an individual cell could be specified by classes spanN, for example, span1, span2, span12. There are also classes offsetN, for example, offset1, offset2, ... offset12, to move cells to the right. A complete reference is available at http://twitter.github.com/bootstrap/scaffolding.html.

We'll use the span12 and hero-unit classes for the main content block:

```
<div class="row-fluid">
  <div class="span12">
    <div id="content">
      <div class="row-fluid">
        <div class="span12">
          <div class="hero-unit">
```

```
<h1>
  Welcome to Super
  Simple Backbone
  Starter Kit
</h1>
<p>
  This is your home page.
  To edit it just modify
  the <i>index.html</i> file!
</p>
<p>
  <a
    class="btn btn-primary btn-large"
    href="http://twitter.github.com/bootstrap"
    target="_blank">
    Learn more
  </a>
</p>
        </div>  <!-- hero-unit -->
      </div>  <!-- span12 -->
    </div> <!-- row-fluid -->
  </div>   <!-- content -->
 </div> <!-- span12 -->
 </div>   <!-- row-fluid -->
```

This is the full source code of the index.html from 1-bootstrap:

```
<!DOCTYPE html>
<html lang="en">
<head>
    <link type="text/css" rel="stylesheet" href="css/bootstrap.css" />
</head>
    <body >
        <div class="container-fluid">
            <div class="row-fluid">
                <div class="span12">
                    <div id="content">
                        <div class="row-fluid">
                            <div class="span12">
                                <div class="hero-unit">
                                    <h1>Welcome to Super Simple Backbone
                                    Starter Kit</h1>
                                    <p>This is your home page. To edit it
                                    just modify <i>index.html</i> file!</p>
                                    <p><a class="btn btn-primary btn-large"
                                    href="http://twitter.github.com/bootstrap"
                                    target="_blank" >Learn more </a></p>
```

49

```
                        </div>  <!-- hero-unit -->
                    </div>  <!-- span12 -->
                </div> <!-- row-fluid -->
            </div>  <!-- content -->
        </div> <!-- span12 -->
      </div>  <!-- row-fluid -->
    </div>  <!-- container-fluid -->
</body>
</html>
```

This example is available for downloading and pulling from the GitHub public repository at github.com/azat-co/fullstack-javascript under the 01-bootstrap folder (https://github.com/azat-co/fullstack-javascript/tree/master/01-bootstrap). If you prefer to watch screencasts, I recorded one on YouTube (http://bit.ly/1RKx9uY).

This and other videos, will walk you through the same steps as outlined in the book. So if you are reading this book in print, no worries. The information in the book is enough.

Here are some other useful tools—CSS frameworks and CSS preprocessors—worth checking out:

- *Compass:* CSS framework (http://compass-style.org/)

- *SASS:* Extension of CSS3 and analog to LESS (http://sass-lang.com/)

- *Blueprint:* CSS framework (http://blueprintcss.org/)

- *Foundation:* Responsive front-end framework (http://foundation.zurb.com/)

- *Bootswatch:* Collection of customized Twitter Bootstrap themes (http://bootswatch.com/)

- *WrapBootstrap:* Marketplace for customized Bootstrap themes (https://wrapbootstrap.com/)

To work with the Twitter Bootstrap source file, you need to use LESS or SASS (another CSS framework similar to LESS).

LESS

LESS is a dynamic stylesheet language. Sometimes, and in this case, it's true that less is more and more is less. A browser cannot interpret LESS syntax, so LESS source code must be compiled to CSS in one of the three ways:

1. In the browser by the LESS JavaScript library

2. On the server side by language or framework; for example, for Node.js there is the LESS module (https://www.npmjs.com/package/less)

3.   Locally on your machine by command line (installed with
     npm by running $ npm install -g less), WinLess
     (http://winless.org/), LESS App
     (http://incident57.com/codekit/index.html), SimpLESS
     (http://wearekiss.com/simpless), or a similar app

The browser option is suitable for a development environment, but suboptimal for a production environment.

Here are some online tools for compilation:

- *LESS2CSS* (http://less2css.org/): A slick, browser-based LESS to CSS converter built on Express.js

- *lessphp* (http://leafo.net/lessphp/): An online demo compiler

- *Dopefly*
  (http://www.dopefly.com/LESS-Converter/less-converter.html):
  An online LESS converter

LESS has variables, mix-ins, and operators that make it faster for developers to reuse CSS rules.

LESS Variables

Variables reduce redundancy and allow developers to change values quickly by having them in one canonical place, and we know that in design (and styling) we often have to change values very frequently.

We sometimes have some LESS code with the variable marked by the @ sign, such as in @color:

```
@color: #4D926F;
#header {
  color: @color;
}
h2 {
  color: @color;
}
```

This code will be compiled to the equivalent in CSS:

```
#header {
  color: #4D926F;
}
h2 {
  color: #4D926F;
}
```

The benefit is that in LESS, you need to update the color value in only one place versus two in CSS. This is abstraction at its best.

51

LESS Mix-ins

This about mix-ins as functions. The syntax for a mix-in is the same as for creating a class selector. For example this is a `.border` mix-in:

```
.border {
    border-top: dotted 1px black;
    border-bottom: solid 2px black;
}
#menu a {
    color: #111;
    .border;
}
.post a {
    color: red;
    .border;
}
```

That converts into this CSS, in which the `.border` is replaced with the actual styles, not the name:

```
.border {
  border-top: dotted 1px black;
  border-bottom: solid 2px black;
}
#menu a {
  color: #111;
  border-top: dotted 1px black;
  border-bottom: solid 2px black;
}
.post a {
  color: red;
  border-top: dotted 1px black;
  border-bottom: solid 2px black;
}
```

Even more useful is to pass a parameter to a mix-in. This enables developers to create even more versatile code. For example, `.rounded-corners` is a mix-in that can change size based on the value of the parameter radius:

```
.rounded-corners (@radius: 5px) {
  border-radius: @radius;
  -webkit-border-radius: @radius;
  -moz-border-radius: @radius;
}
```

```
#header {
  .rounded-corners;
}
#footer {
  .rounded-corners(10px);
}
```

That code will compile into this in CSS:

```
#header {
  border-radius: 5px;
  -webkit-border-radius: 5px;
  -moz-border-radius: 5px;
}
#footer {
  border-radius: 10px;
  -webkit-border-radius: 10px;
  -moz-border-radius: 10px;
}
```

Whether you use mix-ins without parameters or with multiple parameters, they are great at creating abstractions and enabling better code reuse.

LESS Operations

LESS supports operations. With operations, we can perform math functions on numbers, colors, or variables. This is useful for sizing, colors, and other number-related styles.

Here is an example of an operator in LESS where we perform multiplication and addition:

```
@the-border: 1px;
@base-color: #111;
@red:        #842210;

#header {
  color: @base-color * 3;
  border-left: @the-border;
  border-right: @the-border * 2;
}
#footer {
  color: @base-color + #003300;
  border-color: desaturate(@red, 10%);
}
```

That code compiles in this CSS in which the compiler substituted variables and operations for the results of the expressions:

```
#header {
  color: #333333;
  border-left: 1px;
  border-right: 2px;
}
#footer {
  color: #114411;
  border-color: #7d2717;
}
```

As you can see, LESS dramatically improves the reusability of plain CSS. It's a time saver in large projects, as you can create LESS modules and reuse them in multiple apps.

Other important LESS features (http://lesscss.org/#docs) include the following:

- Pattern-matching
- Nested rules
- Functions
- Namespaces
- Scope
- Comments
- Importing

An Example Using a Third-Party API (OpenWeatherMap) and jQuery

Supplemental video which walks you through the implementation and demonstrates the project: http://bit.ly/1RKxyxA.

This example is for purely demonstrative purposes. It is not a part of the main Message Board application covered in later chapters. The goal is to just illustrate the combination of jQuery, JSONP, and REST API technologies.

Note that this example uses OpenWeatherMap API 2.5. The API requires an authentication (an app ID) for REST calls. You can get the necessary keys at openweathermap.org/appid. The API documentation is available at openweathermap.org/api.

The idea of this weather application is to show you an input field for the city name and buttons for metric and imperial systems. Once you enter the city name and click one of the buttons, the app will fetch the forecast from OpenWeatherMap.

In this example, we'll use jQuery's `$.ajax()` function. It has the following syntax:

```
var request = $.ajax({
    url: url,
    dataType: 'jsonp',
    data: {q: cityName, appid: appId, units: units},
    jsonpCallback: 'fetchData',
    type: 'GET'
}).fail(function(error){
    console.error(error)
    alert('Error sending request')
})
```

In the code fragment of an `ajax()` function just shown, we used the following parameters:

- `url` is an endpoint of the API.

- `dataType` is the type of data we expect from the server; for example, "json", "xml", "jsonp" (JSON with prefix—format for servers that don't support CORS).

- `data` is the data to be sent to the server.

- `jsonpCallback` is a name of the function, in a string format, to be called after the request comes back; by default jQuery will create a name.

- `type` is HTTP method of the request; for example, "GET", "POST".

There is also a chained method `.fail`, which has logic for what to do when the request has an error (i.e., it fails).

For more parameters and examples of the `ajax()` function, go to `api.jquery.com/jQuery.ajax`.

To assign our function to a user-triggered event, we need to use the `click` function from the jQuery library. The syntax is very simple:

```
$('#btn').click(function() {
    ...
}
```

`$('#btn')` is a jQuery object that points to an HTML element in the DOM with the id of btn.

To make sure that all of the elements we want to access and use are in the DOM, we need to enclose all of the DOM manipulation code inside of the following jQuery function:

```
$(document).ready(function(){
    ...
}
```

This is a common mistake with dynamically generated HTML elements. They are not available before they have been created and injected into the DOM.

We must put the event handlers for the buttons in the $(document).ready() callback. Otherwise, the code might try to attach an event listener to a nonexisting DOM element. The $(document).ready() ensures that the browser rendered all the DOM elements.

```
$(document).ready(function(){
  $('.btn-metric').click(function() {
    prepareData('metric')
  })
  $('.btn-imperial').click(function() {
    prepareData('imperial')
  })
})
```

We use classes instead of IDs, because classes are more flexible (you cannot have more than one ID with the same name). Here's the HTML code for the buttons:

```
<div class="row">
  <div class="span6 offset1">
    <input type="button" class="btn-primary btn btn-metric"
    value="Get forecast in metric"/>
  <div class="span6 offset1">
    <input type="button" class="btn-danger btn btn-imperial"
    value="Get forecast in imperial"/>
  </div>
  <div class="span3">
    <p id="info"></p>
  </div>
</div>
```

The last container with the ID info is where we'll put the forecast.

The idea is simple: We have button and event listeners to do something once a user clicks the buttons. The aforementioned buttons call the prepareData() method. This is its definition:

```
var openWeatherAppId = 'GET-YOUR-KEY-AT-OPENWEATHERMAP',
  openWeatherUrl = 'http://api.openweathermap.org/data/2.5/forecast'

var prepareData = function(units) {
  var cityName = $('#city-name').val()
  if (cityName && cityName != ''){
    cityName = cityName.trim()
    getData(openWeatherUrl, cityName, openWeatherAppId, units)
  }
  else {
    alert('Please enter the city name')
  }
}
```

The code should be straightforward. We get the value of the city name from the input box, check that it's not empty, and call getDada(), which will make the XHR request to the server. You've already seen an example of the $.ajax request. Please note that the callback function is named fetchData. This function will be called after the browser gets the response from the OpenWeatherMap API. Needless to say, we must pass the city name, app ID, and units as follows:

```
function getData (url, cityName, appId, units) {
  var request = $.ajax({
    url: url,
    dataType: 'jsonp',
    data: {
      q: cityName,
      appid: appId,
      units: units
    },
    jsonpCallback: 'fetchData',
    type: 'GET'
  }).fail(function(error){
    console.error(error)
    alert('Error sending request')
  })
}
```

The JSONP fetching function magically (thanks to jQuery) makes cross-domain calls by injecting script tag, and appending the callback function name to the request query string.

At this point, we need to implement fetchData and update the view with the forecast. The console.log is useful to look up the data structure of the response; that is, where fields are located. The city name and country will be displayed above the forecast to make sure the location found is the same as the one we requested in the input box.

```
function fetchData (forecast) {
    console.log(forecast)
    var html = '',
      cityName = forecast.city.name,
      country = forecast.city.country
```

Now we form the HTML by iterating over the forecast and concatenating the string:

```
html += '<h3> Weather Forecast for '
  + cityName
  + ', '
  + country
  + '</h3>'
forecast.list.forEach(function(forecastEntry, index, list){
  html += '<p>'
```

```
    + forecastEntry.dt_txt
    + ': '
    + forecastEntry.main.temp
    + '</p>'
})
```

Finally, we get a jQuery object for the div with ID `log`, and inject the HTML with the city name and the forecast:

```
$('#log').html(html)
```

In a nutshell, there is a button element that triggers `prepareData()`, which calls `getData()`, in the callback of which is `fetchData()`. If you found that confusing, here's the full code of the `index.html` file:

```html
<!DOCTYPE html>
<html lang="en">
<head>
    <link type="text/css" rel="stylesheet" href="css/bootstrap.css" />
    <script src="js/jquery.js" type="text/javascript"></script>
    <meta name="viewport" content="width=device-width, initial-scale=1.0">
    <script>
        var openWeatherAppId = 'GET-YOUR-KEY-AT-OPENWEATHERMAP',
            openWeatherUrl = 'http://api.openweathermap.org/data/2.5/forecast'

        var prepareData = function(units) {
            var cityName = $('#city-name').val()
            if (cityName && cityName != ''){
                cityName = cityName.trim()
                getData(openWeatherUrl, cityName, openWeatherAppId, units)
            }
            else {
                alert('Please enter the city name')
            }
        }

        $(document).ready(function(){
            $('.btn-metric').click(function() {
                prepareData('metric')
            })
            $('.btn-imperial').click(function() {
                prepareData('imperial')
            })
        })
```

```
function getData (url, cityName, appId, units) {
    var request = $.ajax({
        url: url,
        dataType: 'jsonp',
        data: {
            q: cityName,
            appid: appId,
            units: units
        },
        jsonpCallback: 'fetchData',
        type: 'GET'
    }).fail(function(error){
        console.error(error)
        alert('Error sending request')
    })
}

function fetchData (forecast) {
    console.log(forecast)
    var html = '',
      cityName = forecast.city.name,
        country = forecast.city.country

    html += '<h3> Weather Forecast for '
      + cityName
      + ', '
      + country
      + '</h3>'
    forecast.list.forEach(function(forecastEntry, index, list){
        html += '<p>'
          + forecastEntry.dt_txt
          + ': '
          + forecastEntry.main.temp
          + '</p>'
    })

    $('#log').html(html)
}
    </script>
</head>
<body>

    <div class="container">

        <div class="row">
            <div class="span4 offset 3">
                <h2>Weather App</h2>
                <p>Enter city name to get the weather forecast</p>
            </div>
```

```
                    <div class="span6  offset1"><input class="span4" type="text"
                    placeholder="Enter the city name" id="city-name" value=""/>
                    </div>

            </div>
            <div class="row">
                    <div class="span6 offset1"><input type="button" class="btn-
                    primary btn btn-metric" value="Get forecast in metric"/>
                    <div class="span6 offset1"><input type="button"
                    class="btn-danger btn btn-imperial" value="Get forecast in imperial"/>
                    </div>
                    <div class="span3">
                        <p id="info"></p>
                    </div>
            </div>

            <div class="row">
                    <div class="span6 offset1">
                        <div id="log">Nothing to show yet</div>
                    </div>
            </div>

            <div class="row">
                    <hr/>
                    <p>Azat Mardan (<a href="http://twitter.com/azat_co">@azat_co</a>)</p>
            </div>

        </div>

</body>
</html>
```

Try launching it and see if it works with or without the local HTTP server (just opening index.html in the browser). It should not work without an HTTP server because of its reliance on JSONP technology. You can get http-static or http-server command-line tools as described in Chapter 2.

The source code is available in the 02-weather folder and on GitHub (https://github.com/azat-co/fullstack-javascript/tree/master/02-weather). There's a screencast video on YouTube which walks you through the implementation and demonstrates the app.

This example was built with OpenWeatherMap API v2.5 and might not work with later versions. Also, you need the API key called app ID. You can get the necessary keys at openweathermap.org/appid. If you feel that there must be a working example, please submit your feedback to the GitHub repository for the book's projects (https://github.com/azat-co/fullstack-javascript).

jQuery is a good library for getting data from the RESTful servers. Sometimes we are not just reading the data from the servers; we also want to write it. This way the information persists and can be accessed later. Parse.com will allow you to save your data without friction.

Parse.com

Supplemental video which walks you through the implementation and demonstrates the project: `http://bit.ly/1SU8imX`.

Parse.com (`http://parse.com`) is a service that can be a substitute for a database and a server. It started as means to support mobile application development. Nevertheless, with the REST API and the JavaScript SDK, Parse.com can be used in any web and desktop applications for data storage (and much more), making it ideal for rapid prototyping.

Go to Parse.com and sign up for a free account. Create an application, and copy the Application ID, REST API Key, and JavaScript Key. We'll need these keys to access our collection at Parse.com. Please note the Data Browser tab, as that's where you can see your collections and items.

We'll create a simple application that will save values to the collections using the Parse.com JavaScript SDK. Our application will consist of an `index.html` file and an `app.js` file. Here is the structure of our project folder:

```
/03-parse-sdk
  -index.html
  -app.js
  -jquery.js
  /css
    -boostrap.css
```

The sample is available in the `03-parse-sdk` folder on GitHub (`https://github.com/azat-co/fullstack-javascript/tree/master/03-parse-sdk`), but you are encouraged to type your own code from scratch. To start, create the `index.html` file:

```
<html lang="en">
<head>
```

Include the minified jQuery v2.1.4 library from the local file (you can download and save it into the folder):

```
<script
  type="text/javascript"
  src=
  "jquery.js">
</script>
```

Include the Parse.com JavaScript SDK library v1.6.7 from Parse CDN location:

```
<script
  src="//www.parsecdn.com/js/parse-1.6.7.min.js">
</script>
```

Include our `app.js` file and the Twitter Bootstrap v4.0.0-alpha:

```html
<script type="text/javascript" src="app.js"></script>
<link type="text/css" rel="stylesheet" href="css/bootstrap.css" />
</head>
<body>
<!-- We'll do something here -->
</body>
</html>
```

The `<body>` of the HTML page consists of the `<textarea>` element. We'll use it to enter JSON:

```html
<body>
    <div class="container-fluid">
        <div class="row-fluid">
            <div class="span12">
                <div id="content">
                    <div class="row-fluid">
                        <div class="span12">
                            <div class="hero-unit">
                                <h1>Parse JavaScript SDK demo</h1>
                                <textarea cols="60" rows="7">{
                                  "name": "John",
                                  "text": "hi"
                                }</textarea>
```

The indentation of the `<textarea>` looks out of whack because this element preserves white space and we don't want to have it when we process that string into JSON.

After the input area, there's a button that will trigger the saving to Parse.com:

```html
                                <p><a class="btn btn-primary btn-large
                                btn-save" >Save object</a></p>
                                <pre class="log"></pre>
                                Go to <a href="https://parse.com/apps/"
                                target="_blank">Parse.com</a> to check
                                the data.
                            </div>   <!-- hero-unit -->
                        </div>   <!-- span12 -->
                    </div>   <!-- row-fluid -->
                </div>   <!-- content -->
            </div>   <!-- span12 -->
        </div>   <!-- row-fluid -->
    </div>   <!-- container-fluid -->

</body>
</html>
```

Create the app.js file and use the $(document).ready function to make sure that the DOM is ready for manipulation:

```
$(document).ready(function() {
```

Change parseApplicationId and parseJavaScriptKey to values from the Parse.com application dashboard (you'll need to sign up for the service):

```
var parseApplicationId = 'GET-YOUR-KEYS-AT-PARSE.COM'
var parseJavaScriptKey = 'GET-YOUR-KEYS-AT-PARSE.COM'
```

Because we've included the Parse JavaScript SDK library, we now have access to the global object Parse. We initialize a connection with the keys, and create a reference to a Test collection:

```
  Parse.initialize(parseApplicationId, parseJavaScriptKey)
  var Test = Parse.Object.extend('Test')
  var test = new Test()
```

This simple code will save an object with the keys name and text to the Parse.com Test collection:

```
var Test = Parse.Object.extend('Test')
    var test = new Test()
    $('.btn-save').click(function(){
```

The next few statements deal with getting your JSON from the <textarea> and parsing it into a normal JavaScript object. The try/catch is crucial because the JSON structure is very rigid. You cannot have any extra symbols. Each time there's a syntax error, it will break the entire app. Therefore, we need to account for erroneous syntax:

```
        try {
            var data = JSON.parse($('textarea').val())
        } catch (e) {
            alert('Invalid JSON')
        }
        if (!data) return false
```

Conveniently, the save() method accepts the callback parameters success and error just like the jQuery.ajax() function. To get a confirmation, we'll just have to look at the log container (<pre class="log"></pre>) on the page:

```
  success: function(object) {
    console.log('Parse.com object is saved: ', object)
    $('.log').html(JSON.stringify(object, null, 2))
    // Alternatively you could use alert('Parse.com object is saved')
  },
```

It's important to know why we failed to save an object:

```
error: function(object) {
  console.log('Error! Parse.com object is not saved: ', object)
  }
})
})

})
```

Just so you don't have to click on the Github link (or type it from the book) to look up the full source code of the app.js file, I provide it here:

```
$(document).ready(function() {
    var parseApplicationId = 'GET-YOUR-KEYS-AT-PARSE.COM'
    var parseJavaScriptKey = 'GET-YOUR-KEYS-AT-PARSE.COM'
    // Change parseApplicationId and parseJavaScriptKey to values from
Parse.com application dashboard

    Parse.initialize(parseApplicationId, parseJavaScriptKey)

    var Test = Parse.Object.extend('Test')
    var test = new Test()
    $('.btn-save').click(function(){
        try {
            var data = JSON.parse($('textarea').val())
        } catch (e) {
            alert('Invalid JSON')
        }
        if (!data) return false
        test.save(data, {
        success: function(object) {
          console.log('Parse.com object is saved: ', object)
          $('.log').html(JSON.stringify(object, null, 2))
        },
        error: function(object) {
          console.log('Error! Parse.com object is not saved: ', object)
        }
        })
    })
})
```

We need to use the JavaScript SDK Key from the Parse.com dashboard with this approach. For the jQuery example, we'll be using the REST API Key from the same web page.

To run the app, start your local web server at the project folder and navigate to the address (e.g., http://localhost:8080) in your browser. If you get a 401 Unauthorized error from Parse.com, that's probably because you have the wrong API key.

If everything was done properly, you should be able to see the Test in Parse.com's Data Browser populated with values "John" and "hi". Also, you should see the proper message with the newly created ID. Parse.com automatically creates object IDs and timestamps, which will be very useful in our Message Board application.

Parse.com also has thorough instructions for the Hello World application that are available in the Quick Start Guide sections for new projects (https://parse.com/apps/quickstart#js/blank) and existing ones (https://parse.com/apps/quickstart#js/existing).

Let's move on to the Message Board app.

Message Board with Parse.com Overview

Supplemental video which walks you through the implementation and demonstrates the project: http://bit.ly/1SU8pyS.

The Message Board will consist of an input field, a list of messages, and a send button. We need to display a list of existing messages and be able to submit new messages. We'll use Parse.com as a back end for now, and later switch to Node.js with MongoDB.

You can get a free account at Parse.com. The JavaScript Guide is available at https://parse.com/docs/js_guide and the JavaScript API is available at https://parse.com/docs/js/.

After signing up for Parse.com, go to the dashboard and create a new app if you haven't done so already. Copy your newly created app's Application ID and JavaScript key and REST API key. You will need them later. There are a few ways to use Parse.com:

- *REST API:* We're going to use this approach with the jQuery example.

- *JavaScript SDK:* We just used this approach in our preceding test example, and we'll use it in the Backbone.js example later.

REST API is a more generic approach. Parse.com provides endpoints that we can request with the $.ajax() method from the jQuery library. The description of available URLs and methods can be found at parse.com/docs/rest.

Message Board with Parse.com: REST API and jQuery Version

The full code is available in the 04-board-parse-rest (https://github.com/azat-co/fullstack-javascript/tree/master/04-board-parse-rest) folder, but we encourage you to try to write your own application first.

We'll use Parse.com's REST API and jQuery. Parse.com supports different origin domain AJAX calls, so we won't need JSONP.

When you decide to deploy your back-end application, which will act as a substitute for Parse.com, on a different domain you'll need to use either JSONP on the front end or custom CORS headers on a back end. This topic is covered later in the book.

Right now the structure of the application should look like this:

```
index.html
  css/bootstrap.min.css
  css/style.css
  js/app.js
  img/spinner.gif
```

Let's create a visual representation for the Message Board app. We just want to display a list of messages with names of users in chronological order. Therefore, a table will do just fine, and we can dynamically create `<tr>` elements and keep inserting them as we get new messages.

Create a simple HTML file `index.html` with the following content:

- Inclusion of JS and CSS files

- Responsive structure with Twitter Bootstrap

- A table of messages

- A form for new messages

Let's start with the head and dependencies. We'll include CDN jQuery, local `app.js`, local minified Twitter Bootstrap, and custom stylesheet `style.css`:

```html
<!DOCTYPE html>
<html lang="en">
    <head>
        <script src="js/jquery.js" type="text/javascript"
        language="javascript" ></script>
        <script src="js/app.js" type="text/javascript" language="javascript" >
        </script>
        <link href="css/bootstrap.min.css" type="text/css" rel="stylesheet" />
        <link href="css/style.css" type="text/css" rel="stylesheet" />
        <meta name="viewport" content="width=device-width, initial-scale=1">
    </head>
```

The body element will have typical Twitter Boostrap scaffolding elements defined by classes `container-fluid` and `row-fluid`:

```html
<body>
  <div class="container-fluid">
    <div class="row-fluid">
      <h1>Message Board with Parse REST API</h1>
```

The table of messages is empty, because we'll populate it programmatically from within the JS code:

```html
<table class="table table-bordered table-striped">
  <caption>Messages</caption>
  <thead>
    <tr>
      <th>
        Username
      </th>
      <th>
        Message
      </th>
    </tr>
  </thead>
  <tbody>
    <tr>
      <td colspan="2"><img src="img/spinner.gif" width="20"/></td>
    </tr>
  </tbody>
</table>
</div>
```

Another row and here is our new message form in which the Send button uses Twitter Bootstrap classes btn and btn-primary:

```html
<div class="row-fluid">
  <form id="new-user">
    <input type="text" name="username"
      placeholder="Username" />
    <input type="text" name="message"
      placeholder="Message" />
    <a id="send" class="btn btn-primary">SEND</a>
  </form>
</div>
    </div>
  </body>
</html>
```

The table will contain our messages and the form will provide input for new messages. Now we are going to write three main functions:

1. getMessages(): The function to get the messages

2. updateView(): The function to render the list of messages

3. $('#send').click(...): The function that triggers sending a new message

To keep things simple, we'll put all of the logic in one file app.js. Of course, it a good idea to separate code base on the functionality when your project grows larger.

Replace these values with your own, and be careful to use the REST API key (not the JavaScript SDK key from the previous example):

```
var parseID='YOUR_APP_ID'
var parseRestKey='YOUR_REST_API_KEY'
```

Let's start with document.ready. It will have the logic for fetching messages, and define the Send button's on-click event:

```
$(document).ready(function(){
    getMessages()
    $('#send').click(function(){
```

Let's save the button object:

```
    var $sendButton = $(this)
```

We should show a spinner image ("Loading...") on the button because the request might take some time and we want users to see that our app is working, not just freezing for no apparent reason.

```
        $sendButton.html('<img src="img/spinner.gif" width="20"/>')
        var username = $('input[name=username]').val()
        var message = $('input[name=message]').val()
```

When we submit a new message (a POST request), we make the HTTP call with the jQuery.ajax function. A full list of parameters for the ajax function is available at api.jquery.com/jQuery.ajax. The most important ones are URL, headers, and type parameters.

```
    $.ajax({
      url: ' https://api.parse.com/1/classes/MessageBoard',
      headers: {
        'X-Parse-Application-Id': parseAppID,
        'X-Parse-REST-API-Key': parseRestKey
      },
      contentType: 'application/json',
```

The type of the data is JSON:

```
      dataType: 'json',
      processData: false,
      data: JSON.stringify({
        'username': username,
        'message': message
      }),
```

```
type: 'POST',
success: function() {
  console.log('sent')
```

Assuming the our POST request to Parse saved the new message (success), we now want to get the updated list of messages that will include our message, and replace the spinner image with text as it was before someone clicked the button:

```
      getMessages()
      $sendButton.html('SEND')
    },
    error: function() {
      console.log('error')
      $sendButton.html('SEND')
    }
})
```

To summarize, clicking the Send button will send a POST request to the Parse.com REST API and then, on successful response, get messages calling the getMessages() function.

The getMessages() method to fetch messages from our remote REST API server also uses the jQuery.ajax function. The URL has the name of the collection (MessageBoard) and a query string parameter that sets the limit at 1,000:

```
function getMessages() {
    $.ajax({
        url: ' https://api.parse.com/1/classes/MessageBoard?limit=1000',
```

We need to pass the keys in a header:

```
      headers: {
          'X-Parse-Application-Id': parseAppID,
          'X-Parse-REST-API-Key': parseRestKey
      },
      contentType: 'application/json',
      dataType: 'json',
      type: 'GET',
```

If the request is completed successfully (status 200/ok or similar), we call the updateView function:

```
      success: function(data) {
          console.log('get')
          updateView(data)
      },
      error: function() {
          console.log('error')
      }
  })
}
```

Then, on successful response, it will call the updateView() function, which clears the table tbody and iterates through results of the response using the $.each jQuery function (api.jquery.com/jQuery.each).

This function is rendering the list of messages that we get from the server:

```
function updateView(messages) {
```

We use the jQuery selector .table tbody to create an object referencing that element. Then we clean all the innerHTML of that element:

```
  var table=$('.table tbody')
  table.html('')
```

We use the jQuery.each function to iterate through every message:

```
  $.each(messages.results, function (index, value) {
    var trEl =
```

The following code creates HTML elements (and the jQuery object of those elements) programmatically:

```
      ('<tr><td>'
        + value.username
        + '</td><td>'
        + value.message +
        '</td></tr>')
```

In a sense trEl is a string with HTML for each message or row in the message board. The next line appends (injects after) the table's tbody element our row:

```
    table.append(trEl)
  })
  console.log(messages)
}
```

Here is another way to dynamically create an HTML element (e.g., div) using jQuery:

```
$('<div>')
```

For your reference, here is the entire app.js:

```
var parseAppID='your-parse-app-id'
var parseRestKey='your-rest-api-key'

$(document).ready(function(){
    getMessages()
    $('#send').click(function(){
        var $sendButton = $(this)
        $sendButton.html('<img src="img/spinner.gif" width="20"/>')
        var username = $('input[name=username]').val()
```

```
        var message = $('input[name=message]').val()
        $.ajax({
            url: ' https://api.parse.com/1/classes/MessageBoard',
            headers: {
                'X-Parse-Application-Id': parseAppID,
                'X-Parse-REST-API-Key': parseRestKey
            },
            contentType: 'application/json',
            dataType: 'json',
            processData: false,
            data: JSON.stringify({
                'username': username,
                'message': message
            }),
            type: 'POST',
            success: function() {
                console.log('sent')
                getMessages()
                $sendButton.html('SEND')
            },
            error: function() {
                console.log('error')
                $sendButton.html('SEND')
            }
        })

    })
})
function getMessages() {
    $.ajax({
        url: ' https://api.parse.com/1/classes/MessageBoard?limit=1000',
        headers: {
            'X-Parse-Application-Id': parseAppID,
            'X-Parse-REST-API-Key': parseRestKey
        },
        contentType: 'application/json',
        dataType: 'json',
        type: 'GET',
        success: function(data) {
            console.log('get')
            updateView(data)
        },
        error: function() {
            console.log('error')
        }
    })
}
```

```
function updateView(messages) {
    var table=$('.table tbody')
    table.html('')
    $.each(messages.results, function (index, value) {
        var trEl=('<tr><td>'
            + value.username
            + '</td><td>'
            + value.message
            + '</td></tr>')
        table.append(trEl)
    })

    console.log(messages)
}
```

Try running the code with your local HTTP server. You should see the messages (obviously, there should be no messages for the very first time) and by clicking the button be able to post new ones.

This is fine if all you need to do is develop the app on your local machine, but what about deploying it to the cloud? To do that, we'll need to apply version control with Git first.

Pushing to GitHub

Supplemental video which walks you through the deployment of the project (Git and Heroku part starts at 9minute and 57 seconds): `http://bit.ly/1SU8K4I`.

To create a GitHub repository, go to `github.com`, log in and create a new repository. There will be an SSH address; copy it. In your terminal window, navigate to the project folder that you would like to push to GitHub.

1. Create a local Git and `.git` folder in the root of the project folder:

    `$ git init`

2. Add all of the files to the repository and start tracking them:

    `$ git add .`

3. Make the first commit:

    `$ git commit -am "initial commit"`

4. Add the GitHub remote destination:

    `$ git remote add your-github-repo-ssh-url`

    It might look something like this:

    `$ git remote add origin git@github.com:azat-co/simple-message-board.git`

5. Now everything should be set to push your local Git repository to the remote destination on GitHub with the following command:

```
$ git push origin master
```

6. You should be able to see your files at github.com under your account and repository.

Later, when you make changes to the file, there is no need to repeat all of these steps. Just execute:

```
$ git add .
$ git commit -am "some message"
$ git push origin master
```

If there are no new untracked files you want to start tracking, use this:

```
$ git commit -am "some message"
$ git push origin master
```

To include changes from individual files, run:

```
$ git commit filename -m "some message"
$ git push origin master
```

To remove a file from the Git repository, use:

```
$ git rm filename
```

For more Git commands, see:

```
$ git --help
```

Deploying applications with Windows Azure or Heroku is as simple as pushing code and files to GitHub. The last three steps (4–6) would be substituted with a different remote destination (URL) and a different alias.

Deployment to Windows Azure

You should be able to deploy to Windows Azure with Git using this procedure.

1. Go to the Windows Azure Portal at https://windows.azure.com/1, log in with your Live ID and create a web site if you haven't done so already. Enable Set Up Git Publishing by providing a user name and password (they should be different from your Live ID credentials). Copy your URL somewhere.

2. Create a local Git repository in the project folder that you
    would like to publish or deploy:

    ```
    $ git init
    ```

3. Add all of the files to the repository and start tracking them:

    ```
    $ git add .
    ```

4. Make the first commit:

    ```
    $ git commit -am "initial commit"
    ```

5. Add Windows Azure as a remote Git repository destination:

    ```
    $ git remote add azure your-url-for-remote-repository
    ```

    In my case, this command looked like this:

    ```
    $ git remote add
    > azure https://azatazure@azat.scm.azurewebsites.net/azat.git
    ```

6. Push your local Git repository to the remote Windows Azure
    repository, which will deploy the files and application:

    ```
    $ git push azure master
    ```

As with GitHub, there is no need to repeat the first few steps when you have updated the files later, as we already should have a local Git repository in the form of a .git folder in the root of the project folder.

Deployment to Heroku

Supplemental video which walks you through the deployment of the project (Git and Heroku part starts at 9minute and 57 seconds): http://bit.ly/1SU8K4I.

The only major difference is that Heroku uses Cedar Stack, which doesn't support static projects, including plain HTML applications like our Parse.com test application or Parse.com version of the Message Board application. We can use a "fake" PHP project to get past this limitation. Create a file index.php on the same level as index.html in the project folder, which you would like to publish or deploy to Heroku with the following content:

```php
<?php echo file_get_contents('index.html'); ?>
```

For your convenience, the index.php file is already included in 04-board-parse-rest.

There is an even simpler way to publish static files on Heroku with Cedar Stack, which is described in the post Static Sites on Heroku Cedar (http://kennethreitz.com/static-sites-on-heroku-cedar.html). To make Cedar Stack work with your static files, all you need to do is to type and execute the following commands in your project folder:

```
$ touch index.php
$ echo 'php_flag engine off' > .htaccess
```

Alternatively, you could use the Ruby Bamboo stack. In this case, we would need the following structure:

```
-project folder
  -config.ru
  /public
    -index.html
    -/css
    app.js
    ...
```

The path in index.html to CSS and other assets should be relative, that is 'css/style.css'. The config.ru file should contain the following code:

```
use Rack::Static,
  :urls => ["/stylesheets", "/images"],
  :root => "public"

run lambda { |env|
  [
    200,
    {
      'Content-Type'  => 'text/html',
      'Cache-Control' => 'public, max-age=86400'
    },
    File.open('public/index.html', File::RDONLY)
  ]
}
```

. For more details, you can refer to devcenter.heroku.com/articles/static-sites-on-heroku.

Once you have all of the support files for Cedar Stack or Bamboo, follow these steps:

1. Create a local Git repository and .git folder if you haven't done so already:

   ```
   $ git init
   ```

2. Add files:

   ```
   $ git add .
   ```

3. Commit files and changes:

```
$ git commit -m "my first commit"
```

4. Create the Heroku Cedar Stack application and add the remote destination:

```
$ heroku create
```

If everything went well, it should tell you that the remote has been added and the app has been created, and give you the app name.

5. To look up the remote type and execute (*optional*):

```
$ git remote show
```

6. Deploy the code to Heroku with:

```
$ git push heroku master
```

Terminal logs should tell you whether or not the deployment went smoothly.

7. To open the app in your default browser, type:

```
$ heroku open
```

or just go to the URL of your app, something like `http://yourappname-NNNN.herokuapp.com`.

8. To look at the Heroku logs for this app, type:

```
$ heroku logs
```

To update the app with the new code, repeat the following steps only:

```
$ git add -A
$ git commit -m "commit for deploy to heroku"
$ git push -f heroku
```

You'll be assigned a new application URL each time you create a new Heroku app with the command: `$ heroku create`.

Updating and Deleting Messages

In accordance with the REST API, an update on an object is performed via the PUT method and a delete is performed with the DELETE method. Both of them can easily be performed with the same jQuery.ajax function that we've used for GET and POST, as long as we provide an ID of an object on which we want to execute an operation.

Summary

This chapter was a handful. Hopefully you got some helpful ideas about JSON, AJAX, and cross-domain calls. Remember, when accessing servers you'll need to make sure they support CORS or JSONP.

We've covered some of the meatiest LESS features and worked with Parse to persist the data. We also deployed our app to the cloud using the Git version system.

CHAPTER 4

■ ■ ■

Intro to Backbone.js

Code is not an asset. It's a liability. The more you write, the more you'll have to maintain later.

—Unknown

This chapter will demonstrate:

- Setting up a Backbone.js app from scratch and installing dependencies
- Working with Backbone.js collections
- Backbone.js event binding
- Backbone.js views and subviews with Underscore.js
- Refactoring Backbone.js code
- AMD and Require.js for Backbone.js development
- Require.js for Backbone.js production
- A simple Backbone.js starter kit

Backbone.js has been around for a while so it's very mature and can be trusted to be used in serious front-end development projects. This framework is decidedly minimalistic and unopinionated. You can use Backbone.js with a lot of other libraries and modules. I think of Backbone.js as the foundation to build a custom framework that will be tightly suited to your particular use case.

Some people are turned off by the fact that Backbone.js is unopinionated and minimalistic. They prefer frameworks that do more for them and enforce a particular way of doing things (e.g., the Angular best practices (https://github.com/johnpapa/angular-styleguide)). This is totally fine with me, and you can pursue the study of a more complex front-end framework. They all fit nicely into the Node.js stack and the ecosystem. For the purpose of this book, Backbone.js is ideal because it provides some much needed sanity to the plain nonframework jQuery code, and at the same time it doesn't have a steep learning curve. All you need to know is a few classes and methods, which we cover in this book. Everything else is JavaScript, not a domain-specific language.

Setting Up Backbone.js App from Scratch

We're going to build a typical starter Hello World application using Backbone.js and Mode-View-Controller (MVC) architecture. It might sound like overkill in the beginning, but as we go along we'll add more and more complexity, including models, subviews, and collections.

Full source code for the Hello World app is available under 05-backbone/hello-world and on GitHub (https://github.com/azat-co/fullstack-javascript/tree/master/05-backbone/hello-world).

Backbone.js Dependencies

Supplemental video which walks you through the implementation and demonstrates the project: http://bit.ly/107xRCY.

Download the following libraries:

- jQuery v2.1.4 development source file
  http://code.jquery.com/jquery-2.1.4.js

- Underscore.js v1.8.3 development source file
  http://underscorejs.org/underscore.js

- Backbone.js v1.2.3 development source file
  http://backbonejs.org/backbone.js

Obviously by the time this book is in print, these versions won't be the most recent. I recommend sticking with the versions in this book, because that's what I used to test all the examples and projects. Using different, newer versions might cause some unexpected conflicts.

Create an index.html file, and include these frameworks in this file like this:

```
<!DOCTYPE>
<html>
<head>
  <script src="jquery.js"></script>
  <script src="underscore.js"></script>
  <script src="backbone.js"></script>

  <script>
    // TODO write some awesome JS code!
  </script>

</head>
<body>
</body>
</html>
```

We can also put <script> tags right after the </body> tag at the end of the file. This will change the order in which scripts and the rest of the HTML is loaded, and affect performance in large files.

Let's define a simple Backbone.js router inside of a `<script>` tag:

```
...
var router = Backbone.Router.extend({
})
...
```

For now, to keep it simple (KISS-keep it stupid simple), we'll be putting all of our JavaScript code right into the index.html file. This is not a good idea for a real development or production code, so we'll refactor it later.

Next, set up a special routes property inside of an extend call:

```
var router = Backbone.Router.extend({
  routes: {
  }
})
```

The Backbone.js routes property needs to be in the following format:
'path/:param':'action'

This will result in the filename#path/param URL triggering a function named action (defined in the Router object). For now, we'll add a single home route:

```
var router = Backbone.Router.extend({
  routes: {
    '': 'home'
  }
})
```

This is good, but now we need to add a home function:

```
var router = Backbone.Router.extend({
  routes: {
    '': 'home'
  },
  home: function(){
    // TODO render HTML
  }
})
```

We'll come back to the home function later to add more logic for creating and rendering of a View. Right now we should define our homeView:

```
var homeView = Backbone.View.extend({
})
```

It looks familiar, right? Backbone.js uses similar syntax for all of its components: the extend function and a JSON object as a parameter to it.

There are a multiple ways to proceed from now on, but the best practice is to use the el and template properties, which are special in Backbone.js:

```
var homeView = Backbone.View.extend({
  el: 'body',
  template: _.template('Hello World')
})
```

The property el is just a string that holds the jQuery selector (you can use class name with '.' and id name with '#'). The template property has been assigned an Underscore. js function template with just a plain text 'Hello World.'

To render our homeView we use this.$el, which is a compiled jQuery object referencing element in an el property, and the jQuery .html() function to replace HTML with this.template() value. Here is what the full code for our Backbone.js View looks like:

```
var homeView = Backbone.View.extend({
  el: 'body',
  template: _.template('Hello World'),
  render: function(){
    this.$el.html(this.template({}))
  }
})
```

Now, if we go back to the router we can add these two lines to the home function:

```
var router = Backbone.Router.extend({
  routes: {
    '': 'home'
  },
  initialize: function(){

  },
  home: function(){
    this.homeView = new homeView
    this.homeView.render()
  }
})
```

The first line creates the homeView object and assigns it to the homeView property of the router. The second line will call the render() method in the homeView object, triggering the 'Hello World' output.

Finally, to start a Backbone app, we call new Router inside of a document-ready wrapper to make sure that the file's DOM is fully loaded:

```
var app
$(document).ready(function(){
  app = new router
  Backbone.history.start()
})
```

This time, I won't list the full source code of the index.html because it's rather simple.

Open index.html in the browser to see if it works; that is, the 'Hello World' message should be on the page.

Working with Backbone.js Collections

Supplemental video which walks you through the implementation and demonstrates the project: http://bit.ly/1O7xRCY.

The full source code of this example is under 05-backbone/collections. It's built on top of the "Hello World" example from the Setting up Backbone.js App from Scratch exercise, which is available for download at GitHub (https://github.com/azat-co/fullstack-javascript/tree/master/05-backbone/collections).

We should add some data to play around with, and to hydrate our views. To do this, add this right after the <script> tag and before the other code:

```
var appleData = [
  {
    name: 'fuji',
    url: 'img/fuji.jpg'
  },
  {
    name: 'gala',
    url: 'img/gala.jpg'
  }
]
```

This is our apple *database,* or to be more correct, our REST API endpoint substitute, which provides us with names and image URLs of the apples (data models).

Note that this mock data set can be easily substituted by assigning REST API endpoints of your back end to url properties in Backbone.js collections, models, or both, and calling the fetch() method on them.

Now to make the user experience a little bit better, we can add a new route to the routes object in the Backbone route:

```
...
    routes: {
      '': 'home',
      'apples/:appleName': 'loadApple'
    },
...
```

This will allow users to go to index.html#apples/SOMENAME and expect to see some information about an apple. This information will be fetched and rendered by the loadApple function in the Backbone router definition:

```
loadApple: function(appleName){
  this.appleView.render(appleName)
}
```

Have you noticed an appleName variable? It's exactly the same name as the one that we've used in route. This is how we can access query string parameters (e.g., ?param=value&q=search) in Backbone.js.

Now we'll need to refactor some more code to create a Backbone collection, populate it with data in our appleData variable, and pass the collection to homeView and appleView. Conveniently enough, we do it all in the router constructor method initialize:

```
initialize: function(){
  var apples = new Apples()
  apples.reset(appleData)
  this.homeView = new homeView({collection: apples})
  this.appleView = new appleView({collection: apples})
},
```

At this point, we're pretty much done with the Router class and it should look like this:

```
var router = Backbone.Router.extend({
  routes: {
    '': 'home',
    'apples/:appleName': 'loadApple'
  },
  initialize: function(){
    var apples = new Apples()
    apples.reset(appleData)
    this.homeView = new homeView({collection: apples})
    this.appleView = new appleView({collection: apples})
  },
  home: function(){
    this.homeView.render()
  },
  loadApple: function(appleName){
    this.appleView.render(appleName)
  }
})
```

Let's modify our homeView a bit to see the whole database:

```
var homeView = Backbone.View.extend({
  el: 'body',
  template: _.template('Apple data: <%= data %>'),
  render: function(){
    this.$el.html(this.template({data: JSON.stringify(this.collection.
    models)}))
  }
  // TODO subviews
})
```

For now, we just output the string representation of the JSON object in the browser. This is not user-friendly at all, but later we'll improve it by using a list and subviews.

Our apple Backbone Collection is very clean and simple:

```
var Apples = Backbone.Collection.extend({
})
```

Backbone automatically creates models inside of a collection when we use the fetch() or reset() functions from its API. I find using these functions to be very useful.

Apple View is not any more complex; it has only two properties: template and render. In a template, we want to display figure, img, and figcaption tags with specific values. The Underscore.js template engine is handy at this task:

```
var appleView = Backbone.View.extend({
  template: _.template(
    '<figure>\
      <img src="<%= attributes.url %>"/>\
      <figcaption><%= attributes.name %></figcaption>\
    </figure>'),
...
})
```

To make a JavaScript string that has HTML tags in it more readable, we can use the backslash line breaker escape (\) symbol, or close strings and concatenate them with a plus sign (+). This is an example of appleView earlier, which is refactored using the latter approach:

```
var appleView = Backbone.View.extend({
  template: _.template(
    '<figure>'+
      +'<img src="<%= attributes.url %>"/>'+
      +'<figcaption><%= attributes.name %></figcaption>'+
    +'</figure>'),
...
})
```

Please note the '<%=' and '%>' symbols; they are the instructions for Undescore.js to print values in properties url and name of the attributes object.

Finally, we're adding the render function to the appleView class.

```
render: function(appleName){
```

To get the list of apples filtered by name, there's a where method on the Collection class. We just need the very first item in that array and because arrays in JavaScript are zero-based (they start with a 0 rather than 1 index), the syntax to get the apple model by name is this:

```
var appleModel = this.collection.where({name: appleName})[0]
```

Once we have our model, all we need to do is to pass the model to the template (also called hydrating templates). The result is some HTML that we inject into the <body>:

```
  var appleHtml = this.template(appleModel)
  $('body').html(appleHtml)
}
```

So we find a model within the collection via where() method and use [ ] to pick the first element. Right now, the render function is responsible for both loading the data and rendering it. Later we'll refactor the function to separate these two functionalities into different methods.

For your convenience, here's the whole app, which is in the 05-backbone/ collections/index.html and GitHub (https://github.com/azat-co/fullstack-javascript/blob/master/05-backbone/collections/index.html) folder:

```
<!DOCTYPE>
<html>
<head>
  <script src="jquery.js"></script>
  <script src="underscore.js"></script>
  <script src="backbone.js"></script>

  <script>
    var appleData = [
      {
        name: 'fuji',
        url: 'img/fuji.jpg'
      },
      {
        name: 'gala',
        url: 'img/gala.jpg'
      }
    ]
    var app
    var router = Backbone.Router.extend({
      routes: {
        '': 'home',
        'apples/:appleName': 'loadApple'
      },
      initialize: function(){
        var apples = new Apples()
        apples.reset(appleData)
        this.homeView = new homeView({collection: apples})
        this.appleView = new appleView({collection: apples})
      },
      home: function(){
        this.homeView.render()
      },
```

```
      loadApple: function(appleName){
        this.appleView.render(appleName)
      }
    })

    var homeView = Backbone.View.extend({
      el: 'body',
      template: _.template('Apple data: <%= data %>'),
      render: function(){
        this.$el.html(this.template({data: JSON.stringify(this.collection.
        models)}))
      }
    })

    var Apples = Backbone.Collection.extend({

    })
    var appleView = Backbone.View.extend({
      template: _.template('<figure>\
                              <img src="<%= attributes.url%>"/>\
                              <figcaption><%= attributes.name %></figcaption>\
                            </figure>'),
      render: function(appleName){
        var appleModel = this.collection.where({name: appleName})[0]
        var appleHtml = this.template(appleModel)
        $('body').html(appleHtml)
      }
    })
    $(document).ready(function(){
      app = new router
      Backbone.history.start()
    })

  </script>
</head>
<body>
  <div></div>
</body>
</html>
```

Open collections/index.html file in your browser. You should see the data from our database; that is, Apple data: [{"name":"fuji","url":"img/fuji.jpg"}, {"name":"gala","url":"img/gala.jpg"}].

Now, let' go to collections/index.html#apples/fuji or collections/index.html#apples/gala in your browser. We expect to see an image with a caption. It's a detailed view of an item, which in this case is an apple. Nice work!

Backbone.js Event Binding

Supplemental video which walks you through the implementation and demonstrates the project: http://bit.ly/1kOZnUB.

In real life, getting data does not happen instantaneously, so let's refactor our code to simulate it. For a better user experience (UX), we'll also have to show a loading icon (a spinner or ajax-loader) to users to notify them that the information is being loaded.

It's a good thing that we have event binding in Backbone. Without it, we would have to pass a function that renders HTML as a callback to the data loading function, to make sure that the rendering function is not executed before we have the actual data to display.

Therefore, when a user goes to detailed view (apples/:id) we only call the function that loads the data. Then, with the proper event listeners, our view will automagically (this is not a typo) update itself when there is new data (or on a data change; Backbone.js supports multiple and even custom events).

For your information, if you don't feel like typing out the code (which I recommend), it's in 05-backbone/binding and GitHub (https://github.com/azat-co/fullstack-javascript/blob/master/05-backbone/binding/index.html).

Let's change the code in the router:

```
...
loadApple: function(appleName){
  this.appleView.loadApple(appleName)
}
...
```

Everything else remains the same until we get to the appleView class. We'll need to add a constructor or an initialize method, which is a special word or property in the Backbone.js framework. It's called each time we create an instance of an object, such as var someObj = new SomeObject(). We can also pass extra parameters to the initialize function, as we did with our views (we passed an object with the key collection and the value of apples Backbone Collection). Read more on Backbone.js constructors at backbonejs.org/#View-constructor.

```
...
var appleView = Backbone.View.extend({
  initialize: function(){
    // TODO: create and setup model (aka an apple)
  },
...
```

We have our initialize function; now we need to create a model that will represent a single apple and set up proper event listeners on the model. We'll use two types of events, change and a custom event called spinner. To do that, we are going to use the on() function, which takes these properties: on(event, actions, context). You can read more about it at backbonejs.org/#Events-on.

```
...
var appleView = Backbone.View.extend({
  initialize: function(){
    this.model = new (Backbone.Model.extend({}))
    this.model.bind('change', this.render, this)
    this.bind('spinner', this.showSpinner, this)
  },
  ...
})
...
```

The preceding code basically boils down to two simple things:

1. Call the render() function of the appleView object when the model has changed.

2. Call the showSpinner() method of the appleView object when event spinner has been fired.

So far, so good, right? But what about the spinner, a GIF icon? Let's create a new property in appleView:

```
...
    templateSpinner: '<img src="img/spinner.gif" width="30"/>',
...
```

Remember the loadApple call in the router? This is how we can implement the function in appleView:

```
...
loadApple:function(appleName){
```

To show the spinner GIF image, use this.trigger to make Backbone call the showSpinner:

```
this.trigger('spinner')
```

Next, we'll need to access the context inside of a closure. Sometimes I like to use a meaningful name instead of _this or self, so:

```
var view = this
```

Next, you would have an XHR call (e.g., $.ajax()) to the server to get the data. We'll simulate the real time lag when fetching data from the remote server with:

```
setTimeout(function(){
  view.model.set(view.collection.where({
    name:appleName
  })[0].attributes)
```

```
}, 1000)
},
...
```

The `attributes` is a Backbone.js model property that gives a normal JavaScript object with the model's properties. To summarize, the first line will trigger the `spinner` event (the function for which we still have to write). The second line is just for scoping issues (so we can use `appleView` inside of the closure).

The `setTimeout` function is simulating a time lag of a real remote server response. Inside of it, we assign attributes of a selected model to our view's model by using a `model.set()` function and a `model.attributes` property (which returns the properties of a model).

Now we can remove an extra code from the `render` method and implement the showSpinner function:

```
render: function(appleName){
  var appleHtml = this.template(this.model)
  $('body').html(appleHtml)
},
showSpinner: function(){
  $('body').html(this.templateSpinner)
}
...
```

That's all! Open index.html#apples/gala or index.html#apples/fuji in your browser and enjoy the loading animation while waiting for an apple image to load.

Here is the full code of the index.html file (also in 05-backbone/binding/index. html and https://github.com/azat-co/fullstack-javascript/blob/master/5-backbone/binding/index.html):

```
<!DOCTYPE>
<html>
<head>
  <script src="jquery.js"></script>
  <script src="underscore.js"></script>
  <script src="backbone.js"></script>

  <script>
    var appleData = [
      {
        name: 'fuji',
        url: 'img/fuji.jpg'
      },
      {
        name: 'gala',
        url: 'img/gala.jpg'
      }
    ]
```

```
var app
var router = Backbone.Router.extend({
  routes: {
    '': 'home',
    'apples/:appleName': 'loadApple'
  },
  initialize: function(){
    var apples = new Apples()
    apples.reset(appleData)
    this.homeView = new homeView({collection: apples})
    this.appleView = new appleView({collection: apples})
  },
  home: function(){
    this.homeView.render()
  },
  loadApple: function(appleName){
    this.appleView.loadApple(appleName)

  }
})

var homeView = Backbone.View.extend({
  el: 'body',
  template: _.template('Apple data: <%= data %>'),
  render: function(){
    this.$el.html(this.template({data: JSON.stringify(this.collection.
    models)}))
  }
})

var Apples = Backbone.Collection.extend({
})
var appleView = Backbone.View.extend({
  initialize: function(){
    this.model = new (Backbone.Model.extend({}))
    this.model.on('change', this.render, this)
    this.on('spinner', this.showSpinner, this)
  },
  template: _.template('<figure>\
                        <img src="<%= attributes.url%>"/>\
                        <figcaption><%= attributes.name %></figcaption>\
                      </figure>'),
  templateSpinner: '<img src="img/spinner.gif" width="30"/>',
  loadApple:function(appleName){
    this.trigger('spinner')
    var view = this
    setTimeout(function() {
      view.model.set(view.collection.where({name: appleName})[0].attributes)
```

```
      }, 1000)
    },
    render: function(appleName){
      var appleHtml = this.template(this.model)
      $('body').html(appleHtml)
    },
    showSpinner: function(){
      $('body').html(this.templateSpinner)
    }
  })

  $(document).ready(function(){
    app = new router
    Backbone.history.start()
  })

  </script>
</head>
<body>
  <div></div>
</body>
</html>
```

Backbone.js Views and Subviews with Underscore.js

Supplemental video which walks you through the implementation and demonstrates the project: http://bit.ly/1kOZnUB. And this example is available at https://github.com/azat-co/fullstack-javascript/tree/master/05-backbone/subview.

Subviews are Backbone Views that are created and used inside of another Backbone View. A subviews concept is a great way to abstract (separate) UI events (e.g., clicks), and templates for similarly structured elements (e.g., apples).

A use case of a Subview might include a row in a table, an item in a list, a paragraph, or a new line.

We'll refactor our home page to show a nice list of apples. Each list item will have an apple name and a Buy link with an onClick event. Let's start by creating a subview for a single apple with our standard Backbone extend() function:

```
...
var appleItemView = Backbone.View.extend({
  tagName: 'li',
  template: _.template(''
        +'<a href="#apples/<%=name%>" target="_blank">'
        +'<%=name%>'
        +'</a> <a class="add-to-cart" href="#">buy</a>'),
  events: {
```

```
    'click .add-to-cart': 'addToCart'
  },
  render: function() {
    this.$el.html(this.template(this.model.attributes))
  },
  addToCart: function(){
    this.model.collection.trigger('addToCart', this.model)
  }
})
...
```

Now we can populate the object with tagName, template, events, render, and addToCart properties and methods.

```
...
tagName: 'li',
...
```

tagName automatically allows Backbone.js to create an HTML element with the specified tag name, in this case <li> for list item. This will be a representation of a single apple, a row in our list.

```
...
template: _.template(''
        +'<a href="#apples/<%=name%>" target="_blank">'
        +'<%=name%>'
        +'</a> <a class="add-to-cart" href="#">buy</a>'),
...
```

The template is just a string with Underscore.js instructions. They are wrapped in <% and %> symbols. <%= simply means print a value. The same code can be written with backslash escapes:

```
...
template: _.template('\
        <a href="#apples/<%=name%>" target="_blank">\
        <%=name%>\
        </a> <a class="add-to-cart" href="#">buy</a>\
        '),
...
```

Each <li> will have two anchor elements (<a>), links to a detailed apple view (#apples/:appleName), and a Buy button. Now we're going to attach an event listener to the Buy button:

```
...
events: {
  'click .add-to-cart': 'addToCart'
  },
  ...
```

The syntax follows this rule:

```
event + jQuery element selector: function name
```

Both the key and the value (right and left parts separated by the colon) are strings. For example:

```
'click .add-to-cart': 'addToCart'
```

or

```
'click #load-more': 'loadMoreData'
```

To render each item in the list, we'll use the jQuery `html()` function on the `this.$el` jQuery object, which is the `<li>` HTML element based on our `tagName` attribute:

```
...
render: function() {
  this.$el.html(this.template(this.model.attributes))
},
...
```

`addToCart` will use the `trigger()` function to notify the collection that this particular model (apple) is up for the purchase by the user:

```
...
  addToCart: function(){
    this.model.collection.trigger('addToCart', this.model)
  }
...
```

Here is the full code of the `appleItemView` Backbone View class:

```
...
var appleItemView = Backbone.View.extend({
  tagName: 'li',
  template: _.template(''
        + '<a href="#apples/<%=name%>" target="_blank">'
        + '<%=name%>'
        + '</a> <a class="add-to-cart" href="#">buy</a>'),
  events: {
    'click .add-to-cart': 'addToCart'
  },
  render: function() {
  this.$el.html(this.template(this.model.attributes))
  },
```

```
  addToCart: function(){
    this.model.collection.trigger('addToCart', this.model)
  }
})
...
```

Easy peasy! But what about the master view, which is supposed to render all of our items (apples) and provide a wrapper <ul> container for li HTML elements? We need to modify and enhance our homeView.

To begin with, we can add extra properties of string type understandable by jQuery as selectors to homeView:

```
...
el: 'body',
listEl: '.apples-list',
cartEl: '.cart-box',
...
```

We can use properties from earlier in the template, or just hard-code them (we'll refactor our code later) in homeView:

```
...
template: _.template('Apple data: \
  <ul class="apples-list">\
  </ul>\
  <div class="cart-box"></div>'),
...
```

The initialize function will be called when homeView is created (new homeView()). There we render our template (with our favorite html() function), and attach an event listener to the collection, which is a set of apple models:

```
...
  initialize: function() {
    this.$el.html(this.template)
    this.collection.on('addToCart', this.showCart, this)
  },
...
```

The syntax for the binding event is covered in the previous section. In essence, it is calling the showCart() function of homeView. In this function, we append appleName to the cart (along with a line break, a <br/> element):

```
...
  showCart: function(appleModel) {
    $(this.cartEl).append(appleModel.attributes.name + '<br/>')
  },
...
```

Finally, here is our long-awaited render() method, in which we iterate through each model in the collection (each apple), create an appleItemView for each apple, create an <li> element for each apple, and append that element to view.listEl — <ul> element with a class apples-list in the DOM:

```
...
render: function(){
  view = this
  // So we can use view inside of closure
  this.collection.each(function(apple){
    var appleSubView = new appleItemView({model:apple})
    // Creates subview with model apple
    appleSubView.render()
    // Compiles template and single apple data
    $(view.listEl).append(appleSubView.$el)
    // Append jQuery object from single
    // Apple to apples-list DOM element
  })
}
...
```

Let's make sure we didn't miss anything in the homeView Backbone View. Here's the full code sans the inline comments:

```
...
var homeView = Backbone.View.extend({
  el: 'body',
  listEl: '.apples-list',
  cartEl: '.cart-box',
  template: _.template('Apple data: \
    <ul class="apples-list">\
    </ul>\
    <div class="cart-box"></div>'),
  initialize: function() {
    this.$el.html(this.template)
    this.collection.on('addToCart', this.showCart, this)
  },
  showCart: function(appleModel) {
    $(this.cartEl).append(appleModel.attributes.name + '<br/>')
  },
  render: function(){
    view = this
    this.collection.each(function(apple){
      var appleSubView = new appleItemView({model: apple})
      appleSubView.render()
      $(view.listEl).append(appleSubView.$el)
    })
  }
})
...
```

You should be able to click the Buy button and populate the cart with the apples of your choice. Looking at an individual apple does not require typing its name in the URL address bar of the browser anymore. We can click the name to open a new window with a detailed view.

By using subviews, we reused the template for all of the items (apples) and attached a specific event to each of them (see Figure 4-1). Those events are smart enough to pass the information about the model to other objects: views and collections.

Apple data:

- <u>fuji</u> <u>buy</u>
- <u>gala</u> <u>buy</u>

gala
fuji
fuji
fuji
fuji
fuji
gala
gala
gala
gala
gala

Figure 4-1. *The list of apples rendered by subviews*

Just in case, here is the full code for the subviews example, which is also available at https://github.com/azat-co/fullstack-javascript/blob/master/05-backbone/subview/index.html:

```html
<!DOCTYPE>
<html>
<head>
  <script src="jquery.js"></script>
  <script src="underscore.js"></script>
  <script src="backbone.js"></script>

  <script>
   var appleData = [
      {
        name: 'fuji',
        url: 'img/fuji.jpg'
      },
      {
        name: 'gala',
        url: 'img/gala.jpg'
      }
    ]
    var app
    var router = Backbone.Router.extend({
      routes: {
        '': 'home',
        'apples/:appleName': 'loadApple'
      },
      initialize: function(){
        var apples = new Apples()
        apples.reset(appleData)
        this.homeView = new homeView({collection: apples})
        this.appleView = new appleView({collection: apples})
      },
      home: function(){
        this.homeView.render()
      },
      loadApple: function(appleName){
        this.appleView.loadApple(appleName)

      }
    })
    var appleItemView = Backbone.View.extend({
      tagName: 'li',
      template: _.template('\
              <a href="#apples/<%=name%>" target="_blank">\
              <%=name%>\
```

```
        </a> <a class="add-to-cart" href="#">buy</a>\
        '),

  events: {
    'click .add-to-cart': 'addToCart'
  },
  render: function() {
    this.$el.html(this.template(this.model.attributes))
  },
  addToCart: function(){
    this.model.collection.trigger('addToCart', this.model)
  }
})

var homeView = Backbone.View.extend({
  el: 'body',
  listEl: '.apples-list',
  cartEl: '.cart-box',
  template: _.template('Apple data: \
    <ul class="apples-list">\
    </ul>\
    <div class="cart-box"></div>'),
  initialize: function() {
    this.$el.html(this.template)
    this.collection.on('addToCart', this.showCart, this)
  },
  showCart: function(appleModel) {
    $(this.cartEl).append(appleModel.attributes.name + '<br/>')
  },
  render: function(){
    view = this
    this.collection.each(function(apple){
      var appleSubView = new appleItemView({model: apple})
      appleSubView.render()
      $(view.listEl).append(appleSubView.$el)
    })
  }
})
var Apples = Backbone.Collection.extend({
})
var appleView = Backbone.View.extend({
  initialize: function(){
    this.model = new (Backbone.Model.extend({}))
    this.model.on('change', this.render, this)
    this.on('spinner', this.showSpinner, this)
  },
```

```
      template: _.template('<figure>\
                            <img src="<%= attributes.url%>"/>\
                            <figcaption><%= attributes.name %></figcaption>\
                          </figure>'),
      templateSpinner: '<img src="img/spinner.gif" width="30"/>',
      loadApple:function(appleName){
        this.trigger('spinner')
        var view = this
        setTimeout(function(){
          view.model.set(view.collection.where({name: appleName})[0].attributes)
        }, 1000)
      },
      render: function(appleName){
        var appleHtml = this.template(this.model)
        $('body').html(appleHtml)
      },
      showSpinner: function(){
        $('body').html(this.templateSpinner)
      }
    })

    $(document).ready(function(){
      app = new router
      Backbone.history.start()
    })

  </script>
</head>
<body>
  <div></div>
</body>
</html>
```

The link to an individual item, for example, `collections/index.html#apples/fuji`, also should work independently, by typing it in the browser address bar.

Refactoring Backbone.js Code

Supplemental video which walks you through the implementation and demonstrates the project: `http://bit.ly/1k0ZnUB`.

At this point you are probably wondering what the benefit is of using the framework and still having multiple classes, objects, and elements with different functionalities in one single file. This was done for the purpose of adhering to the idea of keeping things simple.

The bigger your application is, the more pain there is in an unorganized code base. Let's break down our application into multiple files where each file will be one of these types:

- View
- Template
- Router
- Collection
- Model

Let's write these scripts to include tags into our index.html head, or body, as noted previously:

```html
<script src="apple-item.view.js"></script>
<script src="apple-home.view.js"></script>
<script src="apple.view.js"></script>
<script src="apples.js"></script>
<script src="apple-app.js"></script>
```

The names don't have to follow the convention of dashes and dots, as long as it's easy to tell what each file is supposed to do.

Now, let's copy our objects and classes into the corresponding files.

Our main index.html file should look very minimalistic:

```html
<!DOCTYPE>
<html>
<head>
  <script src="jquery.js"></script>
  <script src="underscore.js"></script>
  <script src="backbone.js"></script>

  <script src="apple-item.view.js"></script>
  <script src="apple-home.view.js"></script>
  <script src="apple.view.js"></script>
  <script src="apples.js"></script>
  <script src="apple-app.js"></script>

</head>
<body>
  <div></div>
</body>
</html>
```

The other files just have the code that corresponds to their file names.

The content of apple-item.view.js will have the appleView object:

```
var appleView = Backbone.View.extend({
  initialize: function(){
    this.model = new (Backbone.Model.extend({}))
    this.model.on('change', this.render, this)
    this.on('spinner', this.showSpinner, this)
  },
  template: _.template('<figure>\
            <img src="<%= attributes.url %>"/>\
            <figcaption><%= attributes.name %></figcaption>\
            </figure>'),
  templateSpinner: '<img src="img/spinner.gif" width="30"/>',

  loadApple:function(appleName){
    this.trigger('spinner')
    var view = this
    // We'll need to access that inside of a closure
    setTimeout(function(){
    // Simulates real time lag when fetching
    // data from the remote server
      view.model.set(view.collection.where({
        name: appleName
      })[0].attributes)
    }, 1000)
  },

  render: function(appleName){
    var appleHtml = this.template(this.model)
    $('body').html(appleHtml)
  },
  showSpinner: function(){
    $('body').html(this.templateSpinner)
  }
})
```

The apple-home.view.js file has the homeView object:

```
var homeView = Backbone.View.extend({
  el: 'body',
  listEl: '.apples-list',
  cartEl: '.cart-box',
  template: _.template('Apple data: \
    <ul class="apples-list">\
    </ul>\
```

```
      <div class="cart-box"></div>'),
   initialize: function() {
     this.$el.html(this.template)
     this.collection.on('addToCart', this.showCart, this)
   },
   showCart: function(appleModel) {
     $(this.cartEl).append(appleModel.attributes.name + '<br/>')
   },
   render: function(){
     view = this // So we can use view inside of closure
     this.collection.each(function(apple){
       var appleSubView = new appleItemView({model:apple})
       // Create subview with model apple
       appleSubView.render()
       // Compiles template and single apple data
       $(view.listEl).append(appleSubView.$el)
       // Append jQuery object from
       // single apple to apples-list DOM element
       })
   }
})
```

The `apple.view.js` file contains the master apples list:

```
var appleView = Backbone.View.extend({
   initialize: function(){
     this.model = new (Backbone.Model.extend({}))
     this.model.on('change', this.render, this)
     this.on('spinner',this.showSpinner, this)
   },
   template: _.template('<figure>\
           <img src="<%= attributes.url %>"/>\
           <figcaption><%= attributes.name %></figcaption>\
           </figure>'),
   templateSpinner: '<img src="img/spinner.gif" width="30"/>',
   loadApple:function(appleName){
     this.trigger('spinner')
     var view = this
     // We'll need to access that inside of a closure
     setTimeout(function(){
     // Simulates real time lag when
     // fetching data from the remote server
       view.model.set(view.collection.where({
         name:appleName
       })[0].attributes)
```

```
    }, 1000)
  },
  render: function(appleName){
    var appleHtml = this.template(this.model)
    $('body').html(appleHtml)
  },
  showSpinner: function(){
    $('body').html(this.templateSpinner)
  }
})
```

apples.js is an empty collection:

```
var Apples = Backbone.Collection.extend({
})
```

apple-app.js is the main application file with the data, the router, and the starting command:

```
var appleData = [
  {
    name: 'fuji',
    url: 'img/fuji.jpg'
  },
  {
    name: 'gala',
    url: 'img/gala.jpg'
  }
]
var app
var router = Backbone.Router.extend({
  routes: {
    '': 'home',
    'apples/:appleName': 'loadApple'
  },
  initialize: function(){
    var apples = new Apples()
    apples.reset(appleData)
    this.homeView = new homeView({collection: apples})
    this.appleView = new appleView({collection: apples})
  },
  home: function(){
    this.homeView.render()
  },
```

```
  loadApple: function(appleName){
    this.appleView.loadApple(appleName)
  }
})
$(document).ready(function(){
  app = new router
  Backbone.history.start()
})
```

Now let's try to open the application. It should work exactly the same as in the previous Subviews example.

It's a far better code organization, but it's still far from perfect, because we still have HTML templates directly in the JavaScript code. The problem is that designers and developers can't work on the same files, and any change to the presentation requires a change in the main code base.

We can add a few more JS files to our index.html file:

```
<script src="apple-item.tpl.js"></script>
<script src="apple-home.tpl.js"></script>
<script src="apple-spinner.tpl.js"></script>
<script src="apple.tpl.js"></script>
```

Usually, one Backbone View has one template, but in the case of our appleView—a detailed view of an apple in a separate window—we also have a spinner, a "loading" GIF animation.

The contents of the files are just global variables that are assigned some string values. Later we can use these variables in our views, when we call the Underscore.js helper method _.template().

Here is the apple-item.tpl.js file:

```
var appleItemTpl = '\
    <a href="#apples/<%=name%>" target="_blank">\
    <%=name%>\
    </a> <a class="add-to-cart" href="#">buy</a>\
    '
```

This is the apple-home.tpl.js file:

```
var appleHomeTpl = 'Apple data: \
      <ul class="apples-list">\
      </ul>\
      <div class="cart-box"></div>'
```

Here is the apple-spinner.tpl.js file:

```
var appleSpinnerTpl = '<img src="img/spinner.gif" width="30"/>'
```

This is the apple.tpl.js file:

```
var appleTpl = '<figure>\
                <img src="<%= attributes.url %>"/>\
                <figcaption><%= attributes.name %></figcaption>\
                </figure>'
```

Try to start the application now. The full code is at https://github.com/azat-co/
fullstack-javascript/tree/master/05-backbone/refactor.

As you can see in the previous example, we used global scoped variables (without
the keyword window).

Be careful when you introduce a lot of variables into the global namespace (window
keyword). There might be conflicts and other unpredictable consequences. For example,
if you wrote an open source library and other developers started using the methods and
properties directly, instead of using the interface, what would happen later when you
decide to finally remove or deprecate those global leaks? To prevent this, properly written
libraries and applications use JavaScript closures (https://developer.mozilla.org/en-
US/docs/Web/JavaScript/Closures).

Here is an example of using closure and a global variable module definition:

```
;(function() {
  var apple= function() {
  ...// Do something useful like return apple object
  }
  window.Apple = apple
}())
```

In a case when we need to access the app object (which creates a dependency on
that object):

```
;(function() {
  var app = this.app
  // Equivalent of window.appliation
  // in case we need a dependency (app)
  this.apple = function() {
    ...
    // Return apple object/class
    // Use app variable
  }
  // Equivalent of window.apple = function(){...}
}())
```

As you can see, we've created the function and called it immediately while also
wrapping everything in parentheses ().

AMD and Require.js for Backbone.js Development

Supplemental video which walks you through the implementation and demonstrates the project: `http://bit.ly/1k0ZnUB`.

AMD allows us to organize development code into modules, manage dependencies, and load them asynchronously. This article does a great job at explaining why AMD is a good thing: WHY AMD?

Start your local HTTP server, for example, MAMP (`https://www.mamp.info/en`) or node-static (`https://github.com/cloudhead/node-static`).

Let's enhance our code by using the Require.js library.

Our `index.html` will shrink even more:

```html
<!DOCTYPE>
<html>
<head>
  <script src="jquery.js"></script>
  <script src="underscore.js"></script>
  <script src="backbone.js"></script>
  <script src="require.js"></script>
  <script src="apple-app.js"></script>
</head>
<body>
  <div></div>
</body>
</html>
```

We only included libraries and the single JavaScript file with our application. This file has the following structure:

```
require([...],function(...){...})
```

In a more explanatory way:

```
require([
  'name-of-the-module',
  ...
  'name-of-the-other-module'
  ],function(referenceToModule, ..., referenceToOtherModule){
  ...// Some useful code
  referenceToModule.someMethod()
})
```

Basically, we tell a browser to load the files from the array of file names—the first parameter of the require() function—and then pass our modules from those files to the anonymous callback function (second argument) as variables. Inside of the main function (anonymous callback) we can use our modules by referencing those variables. Therefore, our apple-app.js metamorphoses into:

```
require([
  'apple-item.tpl', // Can use shim plug-in
  'apple-home.tpl',
  'apple-spinner.tpl',
  'apple.tpl',
  'apple-item.view',
  'apple-home.view',
  'apple.view',
  'apples'
],function(
  appleItemTpl,
  appleHomeTpl,
  appleSpinnerTpl,
  appleTpl,
  appelItemView,
  homeView,
  appleView,
  Apples
  ){
  var appleData = [
    {
      name: 'fuji',
      url: 'img/fuji.jpg'
    },
    {
      name: 'gala',
      url: 'img/gala.jpg'
    }
  ]
  var app
  var router = Backbone.Router.extend({
  // Check if need to be required
    routes: {
      '': 'home',
      'apples/:appleName': 'loadApple'
    },
    initialize: function(){
      var apples = new Apples()
      apples.reset(appleData)
      this.homeView = new homeView({collection: apples})
```

```
        this.appleView = new appleView({collection: apples})
      },
      home: function(){
        this.homeView.render()
      },
      loadApple: function(appleName){
        this.appleView.loadApple(appleName)
      }
    })

    $(document).ready(function(){
      app = new router
      Backbone.history.start()
    })
  })
```

We put all of the code inside the function that is a second argument of `require()`, mentioned modules by their file names, and used dependencies via corresponding parameters. Now we should define the module itself. This is how we can do it with the `define()` method:

```
define([...],function(...){...})
```

The meaning is similar to the `require()` function: Dependencies are strings of file names (and paths) in the array that is passed as the first argument. The second argument is the main function that accepts other libraries as parameters (the order of parameters and modules in the array is important):

```
define(['name-of-the-module'],function(nameOfModule){
  var b = nameOfModule.render()
  return b
})
```

Note that there is no need to append `.js` to file names. Require.js does it automatically. The Shim plug-in is used for importing text files such as HTML templates.

Let's start with the templates and convert them into the Require.js modules.

Here is the new `apple-item.tpl.js` file:

```
define(function() {
  return '\
            <a href="#apples/<%=name%>" target="_blank">\
            <%=name%>\
            </a> <a class="add-to-cart" href="#">buy</a>\
            '
})
```

This is the apple-home.tpl file:

```
define(function(){
  return 'Apple data: \
        <ul class="apples-list">\
        </ul>\
        <div class="cart-box"></div>'
})
```

Here is the apple-spinner.tpl.js file:

```
define(function(){
  return '<img src="img/spinner.gif" width="30"/>'
})
```

This is the apple.tpl.js file:

```
define(function(){
  return '<figure>\
        <img src="<%= attributes.url %>"/>\
        <figcaption><%= attributes.name %></figcaption>\
        </figure>'
 })
```

Here is the apple-item.view.js file:

```
define(function() {
  return '\
          <a href="#apples/<%=name%>" target="_blank">\
          <%=name%>\
          </a> <a class="add-to-cart" href="#">buy</a>\
          '
})
```

In the apple-home.view.js file, we need to declare dependencies on apple-home.tpl and apple-item.view.js files:

```
define(['apple-home.tpl', 'apple-item.view'], function(
  appleHomeTpl,
  appleItemView){
return  Backbone.View.extend({
      el: 'body',
      listEl: '.apples-list',
      cartEl: '.cart-box',
      template: _.template(appleHomeTpl),
```

```
    initialize: function() {
      this.$el.html(this.template)
      this.collection.on('addToCart', this.showCart, this)
    },
    showCart: function(appleModel) {
      $(this.cartEl).append(appleModel.attributes.name + '<br/>')
    },
    render: function(){
      view = this // So we can use view inside of closure
      this.collection.each(function(apple){
        var appleSubView = new appleItemView({model:apple})
        // Create subview with model apple
        appleSubView.render()
        // Compiles template and single apple data
        $(view.listEl).append(appleSubView.$el)
        // Append jQuery object from
        // a single apple to apples-list DOM element
      })
    }
  })
})
```

The apple.view.js file depends on two templates:

```
define([
  'apple.tpl',
  'apple-spinner.tpl'
], function(appleTpl,appleSpinnerTpl){
  return  Backbone.View.extend({
    initialize: function(){
      this.model = new (Backbone.Model.extend({}))
      this.model.on('change', this.render, this)
      this.on('spinner',this.showSpinner, this)
    },
    template: _.template(appleTpl),
    templateSpinner: appleSpinnerTpl,
    loadApple:function(appleName){
      this.trigger('spinner')
      var view = this
      // We'll need to access that inside of a closure
      setTimeout(function(){
      // Simulates real time lag when
      // fetching data from the remote server
        view.model.set(view.collection.where({
          name:appleName
        })[0].attributes)
      }, 1000)
    },
```

```
    render: function(appleName){
      var appleHtml = this.template(this.model)
      $('body').html(appleHtml)
    },
    showSpinner: function(){
      $('body').html(this.templateSpinner)
    }
  })
})
```

This is the `apples.js` file:

```
define(function(){
  return Backbone.Collection.extend({})
})
```

I hope you can see the pattern by now. All of our code is split into the separate files based on the logic (e.g., view class, collection class, template). The main file loads all of the dependencies with the `require()` function. If we need some module in a nonmain file, then we can ask for it in the `define()` method. Usually, in modules we want to return an object; for example, in templates we return strings and in views we return Backbone View classes and objects.

Try launching the example located at `https://github.com/azat-co/fullstack-javascript/blob/master/05-backbone/amd/`. Visually, there shouldn't be any changes. If you open the Network tab in the Developers Tool, you can see a difference in how the files are loaded.

The old file shown in Figure 4-2 (`https://github.com/azat-co/fullstack-javascript/tree/master/05-backbone/refactor/index.html`) loads our JavaScript scripts in a serial manner, whereas the new file shown in Figure 4-3 (`https://github.com/azat-co/fullstack-javascript/blob/master/05-backbone/amd/index.html`) loads them in parallel.

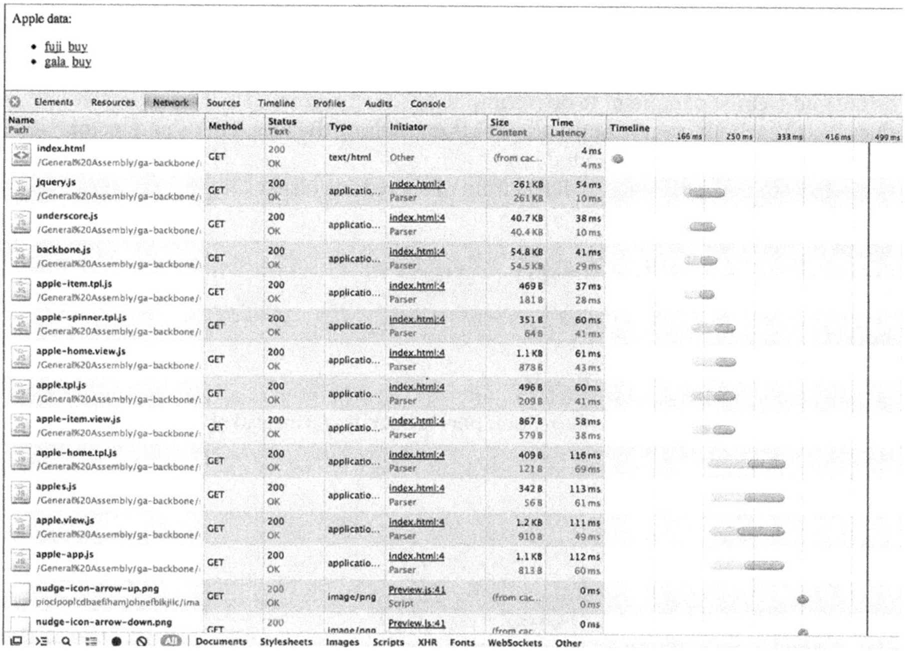

Figure 4-2. *The old 05-backbone/refactor/index.html file*

Figure 4-3. *The new 05-backbone/amd/index.html file*

Require.js has a lot of configuration options that are defined through the `requirejs.config()` call in the top level of an HTML page. More information can be found at requirejs.org/docs/api.html#config.

Let's add a bust parameter to our example. The bust argument will be appended to the URL of each file, preventing a browser from caching the files. This is perfect for development and terrible for production.

Add this to the `apple-app.js` file in front of everything else:

```
requirejs.config({
  urlArgs: 'bust=' + (new Date()).getTime()
})
require([
...
```

Notice in Figure 4-4 that each file request now has status 200 instead of 304 (not modified).

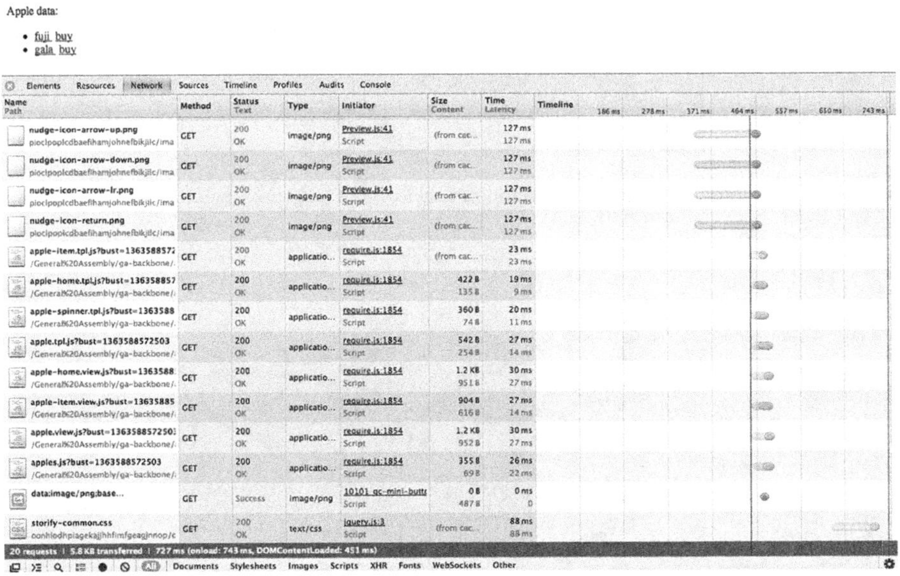

Figure 4-4. *Network tab with bust parameter added*

Require.js for Backbone.js Production

We'll use the Node Package Manager (NPM) to install the requirejs library (it's not a typo; there's no period in the name). In your project folder, run this command in a terminal:

```
$ npm init
```

Then run

```
$ npm install requirejs
```

or add -g for global installation:

```
$ npm install -g requirejs
```

Create a file named app.build.js:

```
({
    appDir: "./js",
    baseUrl: "./",
    dir: "build",
    modules: [
        {
            name: "apple-app"
        }
    ]
})
```

Move the script files into the js folder (appDir property). The builded files will be placed in the build folder (dir parameter). For more information on the build file, check out the extensive example with comments available at https://github.com/jrburke/r.js/blob/master/build/example.build.js.

Now everything should be ready for building one gigantic JavaScript file that will include all of our dependencies and modules:

```
$ r.js -o app.build.js
```

or

```
$ node_modules/requirejs/bin/r.js -o app.build.js
```

You should get a list of the r.js processed files, as shown in Figure 4-5.

```
Uglifying file: /Users/azat/Documents/Development/General Assembly/ga-backbone/r/build/apple-app.js
Uglifying file: /Users/azat/Documents/Development/General Assembly/ga-backbone/r/build/apple-home.tpl.js
Uglifying file: /Users/azat/Documents/Development/General Assembly/ga-backbone/r/build/apple-home.view.js
Uglifying file: /Users/azat/Documents/Development/General Assembly/ga-backbone/r/build/apple-item.tpl.js
Uglifying file: /Users/azat/Documents/Development/General Assembly/ga-backbone/r/build/apple-item.view.js
Uglifying file: /Users/azat/Documents/Development/General Assembly/ga-backbone/r/build/apple-spinner.tpl.js
Uglifying file: /Users/azat/Documents/Development/General Assembly/ga-backbone/r/build/apple.tpl.js
Uglifying file: /Users/azat/Documents/Development/General Assembly/ga-backbone/r/build/apple.view.js
Uglifying file: /Users/azat/Documents/Development/General Assembly/ga-backbone/r/build/apples.js
Uglifying file: /Users/azat/Documents/Development/General Assembly/ga-backbone/r/build/backbone.js
Uglifying file: /Users/azat/Documents/Development/General Assembly/ga-backbone/r/build/jquery.js
toTransport skipping /Users/azat/Documents/Development/General Assembly/ga-backbone/r/build/node_modules/.bin/r.js: Error: Line 1: Unexpe
cted token ILLEGAL
Error: Cannot parse file: /Users/azat/Documents/Development/General Assembly/ga-backbone/r/build/node_modules/.bin/r.js for comments. Ski
pping it. Error is:
Error: Line 1: Unexpected token ILLEGAL
toTransport skipping /Users/azat/Documents/Development/General Assembly/ga-backbone/r/build/node_modules/requirejs/bin/r.js: Error: Line
1: Unexpected token ILLEGAL
Error: Cannot parse file: /Users/azat/Documents/Development/General Assembly/ga-backbone/r/build/node_modules/requirejs/bin/r.js for comm
ents. Skipping it. Error is:
Error: Line 1: Unexpected token ILLEGAL
Uglifying file: /Users/azat/Documents/Development/General Assembly/ga-backbone/r/build/node_modules/requirejs/require.js
Uglifying file: /Users/azat/Documents/Development/General Assembly/ga-backbone/r/build/require.js
Uglifying file: /Users/azat/Documents/Development/General Assembly/ga-backbone/r/build/underscore.js

apple-app.js
------------------
apple-item.tpl.js
apple-home.tpl.js
apple-spinner.tpl.js
apple.tpl.js
apple-item.view.js
apple-home.view.js
apple.view.js
apples.js
apple-app.js

● r git:(master) ✗ $ node_modules/requirejs/bin/r.js -o app.build.js|
```

Figure 4-5. *A list of the r.js processed files*

Open index.html from the build folder in a browser window, and check if the Network tab shows any improvement now with just one request or file to load (Figure 4-6).

Figure 4-6. *Performance improvement with one request or file to load*

For more information, check out the official r.js documentation at requirejs.org/docs/optimization.html.

The example code is available at https://github.com/azat-co/fullstack-javascript/tree/master/05-backbone/r and https://github.com/azat-co/fullstack-javascript/tree/master/05-backbone/r/build.

For uglification of JS files (which decreases the file sizes), we can use the Uglify2 module. To install it with NPM, use:

```
$ npm install uglify-js
```

Then update the app.build.js file with the optimize: "uglify2" property:

```
({
    appDir: "./js",
    baseUrl: "./",
    dir: "build",
    optimize: "uglify2",
    modules: [
        {
            name: "apple-app"
        }
    ]
})
```

Run r.js with:

```
$ node_modules/requirejs/bin/r.js -o app.build.js
```

You should get something like this:

```
define("apple-item.tpl",[],function(){return' <a href="#apples/<%=name%>"
target="_blank"> <%=name%> </a> <a class="add-to-cart" href="#">buy</a>
'}),define("apple-home.tpl",[],function(){return'Apple data:<ulclass=
"apples-list"></ul><div class="cart-box"></div>'}),define("apple-spinner.tpl",
[],function(){return'<img src="img/spinner.gif" width="30"/>'}),define(
"apple.tpl",[],function(){return'<figure><img src="<%= attributes.url %>"/>
<figcaption><%= attributes.name %></figcaption></figure>'}),define("apple-
item.view",["apple-item.tpl"],function(e){return Backbone.View.extend({tagName:
"li",template:_.template(e),events:{"click .add-to-cart":"addToCart"},
render:function(){this.$el.html(this.template(this.model.attributes))},
addToCart:function(){this.model.collection.trigger("addToCart",this.model)}})}),
define("apple-home.view",["apple-home.tpl","apple-item.view"],function(e,t)
{return Backbone.View.extend({el:"body",listEl:".apples-list",cartEl:
".cart-box",template:_.template(e),initialize:function(){this.$el.html(this.
template),this.collection.on("addToCart",this.showCart,this)},showCart:
function(e){$(this.cartEl).append(e.attributes.name+"<br/>")},render:
function(){view=this,this.collection.each(function(e){var i=new t({model:e});
i.render(),$(view.listEl).append(i.$el)})}})}),define("apple.view",
```

```
["apple.tpl","apple-spinner.tpl"],function(e,t){return Backbone.View.extend
({initialize:function(){this.model=new(Backbone.Model.extend({})),this.
model.on("change",this.render,this),this.on("spinner",this.showSpinner,
this)},template:_.template(e),templateSpinner:t,loadApple:function(e)
{this.trigger("spinner");var t=this;setTimeout(function(){t.model.set(t.
collection.where({name:e})[0].attributes)},1e3)},render:function()
{var e=this.template(this.model);$("body").html(e)},showSpinner:function()
{$("body").html(this.templateSpinner)}})}),define("apples",[],function()
{return Backbone.Collection.extend({})}),requirejs.config({urlArgs:
"bust="+(new Date).getTime()}),require(["apple-item.tpl","apple-home.tpl",
"apple-spinner.tpl","apple.tpl","apple-item.view","apple-home.view",
"apple.view","apples"],function(e,t,i,n,a,l,p,o){var r,s=[{name:"fuji",
url:"img/fuji.jpg"},{name:"gala",url:"img/gala.jpg"}],c=Backbone.Router.
extend({routes:{"":"home","apples/:appleName":"loadApple"},initialize:
function(){var e=new o;e.reset(s),this.homeView=new l({collection:e}),
this.appleView=new p({collection:e})},home:function(){this.homeView.
render()},loadApple:function(e){this.appleView.loadApple(e)}});$(document).
ready(function(){r=new c,Backbone.history.start()})}),define("apple-app",
function(){});
```

The file is intentionally not formatted to show how Uglify2
(https://github.com/mishoo/UglifyJS2) works. Without the line break escape symbols,
the code is on one line. Also notice that variables' and objects' names are shortened.

Super Simple Backbone.js Starter Kit

To jump-start your Backbone.js development, consider using Super Simple Backbone
Starter Kit (https://github.com/azat-co/super-simple-backbone-starter-kit) or
similar projects:

- Backbone Boilerplate available at http://backboneboilerplate.com/

- Sample App with Backbone.js and Twitter Bootstrap available
  at http://coenraets.org/blog/2012/02/sample-app-with-
  backbone-js-and-twitter-bootstrap/

- More Backbone.js tutorials available at github.com/
  documentcloud/backbone/wiki/Tutorials%2C-blog-posts-and-
  example-sites

Summary

So far we've covered how to:

- Build a Backbone.js application from scratch.

- Use views, collections, subviews, models, and event binding.

- Use AMD and Require.js on the example of the apple database application.

In this chapter, you've learned enough about Backbone.js to make sure you can start using it in your web or mobile apps. Without a framework like Backbone, your code will become exponentially more complex as it grows. On the other hand, with Backbone or a similar MVC, you can scale the code better.

CHAPTER 5

▦ ▦ ▦

Backbone.js and Parse.com

Java is to JavaScript what Car is to Carpet.

—Chris Heilmann

In this chapter, we'll explore the practical aspect of leveraging Parse.com for a Backbone.js app. The chapter will illustrate the Backbone.js uses with Parse.com and its JavaScript SDK on the modified Message Board app.

If you've written some complex client-side applications, you might have found that it's challenging to maintain the spaghetti code of JavaScript callbacks and UI events. Backbone.js provides a lightweight yet powerful way to organize your logic into a Model-View-Controller (MVC) type of structure. It also has nice features like URL routing, REST API support, event listeners, and triggers. For more information and step-by-step examples of building Backbone.js applications from scratch, please refer to the chapter "Intro to Backbone.js."

Message Board with Parse.com: JavaScript SDK and Backbone.js Version

Supplemental video which walks you through the implementation and demonstrates the project: `http://bit.ly/1QnqsQC`.

It's easy to see that if we keep adding more and more buttons such as "DELETE," "UPDATE," and other functionalities, our system of asynchronous callback will grow more complicated. And we'll have to know when to update the view (i.e., the list of messages) based on whether or not there were changes to the data. The Backbone.js Model-View-Controller (MVC) framework can be used to make complex applications more manageable and easier to maintain.

If you felt comfortable with the previous example, let's build upon it with the use of the Backbone.js framework. Here we'll go step by step, creating a Message Board application using Backbone.js and Parse.com JavaScript SDK. If you feel familiar enough with it, you could download the Super Simple Backbone Starter Kit at `github.com/azat-co/super-simple-backbone-starter-kit`. Integration with Backbone.js will allow for a straightforward implementation of user actions by binding them to asynchronous updates of the collection.

The application is available at https://github.com/azat-co/fullstack-javascript/tree/master/06-board-backbone-parse-sdk, but again you are encouraged to start from scratch and try to write your own code using the example only as a reference.

The following shows the structure of Message Board with Parse.com, JavaScript SDK, and Backbone.js version:

```
/06-board-backbone-parse-sdk
  -index.html
  -home.html
  -footer.html
  -header.html
  -app.js
  /css
    -bootstrap.css
    -bootstrap.min.css
  /js
    -backbone.js
    -jquery.js
    -underscore.js
  /libs
    -require.min.js
    -text.js
```

Create a folder; in the folder create an index.html file with the following content skeleton:

```html
<!DOCTYPE html>
<html lang="en">
  <head>

    ...

  </head>
  <body>

    ...

  </body>
</html>
```

Download the necessary libraries or hot-link them from Google API. Now include JavaScript libraries and Twitter Bootstrap style sheets into the head element along with other important but not required *meta* elements.

```html
<head>
  <meta charset="utf-8" />
  <title>Message Board</title>
  <meta name="author" content="Azat Mardan" />
```

We need this for responsive behavior:

```
<meta name="viewport"
  content="width=device-width, initial-scale=1.0" />
```

Link jQuery v2.1.4 from a local file:

```
<script src="js/jquery.js"></script>
```

Do the same for Underscore v1.8.3 and Backbone v1.2.3:

```
<script src="js/underscore.js"></script>
<script src="js/backbone.js"></script>
```

The Parse JavaScript SDK v1.5.0 is hot-linked from Parse.com CDN. Note the version number, because the older versions might not work properly with this example:

```
<script src="//www.parsecdn.com/js/parse-1.5.0.min.js"></script>
```

Twitter Bootstrap CSS inclusion:

```
<link type="text/css" rel="stylesheet" href="css/bootstrap.css" />
```

We need to have RequireJS v2.1.22 for loading dependencies:

```
<script type="text/javascript" src="libs/require.js"></script>
```

And here's our JS application inclusion:

```
<script type="text/javascript" src="app.js"></script>
</head>
```

Populate the <body> element with Twitter Bootstrap scaffolding (more about it in the "Basics" chapter):

```
<body>
<div class="container-fluid">
  <div class="row-fluid">
    <div class="span12">
      <div id="header">
      </div>
    </div>
  </div>
  <div class="row-fluid">
    <div class="span12">
      <div id="content">
      </div>
```

```html
      </div>
    </div>
    <div class="row-fluid">
      <div class="span12">
        <div id="footer">
        </div>
      </div>
    </div>
  </div>
</body>
```

Create an app.js file and put Backbone.js views inside:

- headerView: menu and app-common information

- footerView: copyrights and contact links

- homeView: home page content

We use Require.js syntax and shim plugin for HTML templates:

```javascript
require([
'libs/text!header.html',
'libs/text!home.html',
'libs/text!footer.html'], function (
headerTpl,
homeTpl,
footerTpl) {
```

The application router with a single index route:

```javascript
var ApplicationRouter = Backbone.Router.extend({
  routes: {
    "": "home",
    "*actions": "home"
  },
```

Before we do anything else, we can initialize views that are going to be used across the app:

```javascript
initialize: function() {
  this.headerView = new HeaderView()
  this.headerView.render()
  this.footerView = new FooterView()
  this.footerView.render()
},
```

This code takes care of the home route:

```
home: function() {
  this.homeView = new HomeView()
  this.homeView.render()
}
})
```

The header Backbone View is attached to the #header element and uses the headerTpl template:

```
HeaderView = Backbone.View.extend({
  el: '#header',
  templateFileName: 'header.html',
  template: headerTpl,
  initialize: function() {
  },
  render: function() {
    console.log(this.template)
    $(this.el).html(_.template(this.template))
  }
})
```

To render the HTML, we use the jQuery.html() function:

```
FooterView = Backbone.View.extend({
  el: '#footer',
  template: footerTpl,
  render: function() {
    this.$el.html(_.template(this.template))
  }
})
```

The home Backbone View definition uses the #content DOM element:

```
HomeView = Backbone.View.extend({
  el: '#content',
  template: homeTpl,
  initialize: function() {
  },
  render: function() {
    $(this.el).html(_.template(this.template))
  }
})
```

To start an app, we create a new instance and call `Backbone.history.start()`:

```
app = new ApplicationRouter()
Backbone.history.start()
})
```

The full code of the `app.js` file:

```
require([
    'libs/text!header.html',
    // Example of a shim plugin use
    'libs/text!home.html',
    'libs/text!footer.html'],
  function (
    headerTpl,
    homeTpl,
    footerTpl) {
  var ApplicationRouter = Backbone.Router.extend({
    routes: {
      '': 'home',
      '*actions': 'home'
    },
    initialize: function() {
      this.headerView = new HeaderView()
      this.headerView.render()
      this.footerView = new FooterView()
      this.footerView.render()
    },
    home: function() {
      this.homeView = new HomeView()
      this.homeView.render()
    }
  })
  HeaderView = Backbone.View.extend({
    el: '#header',
    templateFileName: 'header.html',
    template: headerTpl,
    initialize: function() {
    },
    render: function() {
      console.log(this.template)
      $(this.el).html(_.template(this.template))
    }
  })
```

```
FooterView = Backbone.View.extend({
  el: '#footer',
  template: footerTpl,
  render: function() {
    this.$el.html(_.template(this.template))
  }
})

HomeView = Backbone.View.extend({
  el: '#content',
  template: homeTpl,
  initialize: function() {
  },
  render: function() {
    $(this.el).html(_.template(this.template))
  }
})

app = new ApplicationRouter()
Backbone.history.start()
})
```

The code above displays templates. All views and routers are inside, requiring the module to make sure that the templates are loaded before we begin to process them.

Here is what home.html looks like:

- A table of messages

- Underscore.js logic to output rows of the table

- A new message form

Let's use the Twitter Bootstrap library structure (with its responsive components) by assigning row-fluid and span12 classes:

```
<div class="row-fluid"  id="message-board">
<div class="span12">
  <table class="table table-bordered table-striped">
    <caption>Message Board</caption>
    <thead>
      <tr>
        <th class="span2">Username</th>
        <th>Message</th>
      </tr>
    </thead>
    <tbody>
```

This part has Underscore.js template instructions, which are just some JS code wrapped in <% and %> marks. Right away we are checking that the models variable is defined and not empty:

```
<%
if (typeof models != 'undefined' && models.length > 0) {
```

_.each() is an iteration function from the UnderscoreJS library (underscorejs. org/#each), which does exactly what it sounds like—iterates through elements of an object/array:

```
_.each(models, function (value, key, list) { %>
  <tr>
```

Inside of the iterator function we have value that is a model. We can access Backbone model's attributes with model.attributes.attributeName. To output variables in Underscore, we use <%= NAME %> instead of <% CODE %>:

```
      <td><%= value.attributes.username %></td>
      <td><%= value.attributes.message %></td>
    </tr>
  <% })
}
```

But what if models is undefined or empty? In this case, we print a message that says that there's no messages yet. It goes into the else block. We use colspan=2 to merge two cells into one:

```
      else { %>
      <tr>
        <td colspan="2">No messages yet</td>
      </tr>
```

We close the table and other HTML tags:

```
      <%}%>
      </tbody>
    </table>
  </div>
</div>
```

For the new message form, we also use the row-fluid class and then add <input> elements:

```
<div class="row-fluid" id="new-message">
  <div class="span12">
    <form class="well form-inline">
```

The input element must have the name username because that's how we find this element and get the username value in the JavaScript code:

```html
<input type="text"
  name="username"
  class="input-small"
  placeholder="Username" />
```

Analogous to the username <input> tag, the message text tag needs to have the name. In this case, it's message:

```html
<input type="text" name="message"
  class="input-small"
  placeholder="Message Text" />
```

Lastly, the send button must have the ID of send. This is what we use in the Backbone's events property on the HomeView class:

```html
    <a id="send" class="btn btn-primary">SEND</a>
  </form>
  </div>
</div>
```

For your convenience, here's the full code of the home.html template file:

```html
<div class="row-fluid"  id="message-board">
<div class="span12">
  <table class="table table-bordered table-striped">
    <caption>Message Board</caption>
    <thead>
      <tr>
        <th class="span2">Username</th>
        <th>Message</th>
      </tr>
    </thead>
    <tbody>
      <% if (typeof models != 'undefined' && models.length>0) {
        _.each(models, function (value, key, list) { %>
          <tr>
            <td><%= value.attributes.username %></td>
            <td><%= value.attributes.message %></td>
          </tr>
        <% })
      }
      else { %>
      <tr>
        <td colspan="2">No messages yet</td>
      </tr>
```

```
      <%}%>
    </tbody>
  </table>
</div>
</div>
<div class="row-fluid"  id="new-message">
  <div class="span12">
    <form class="well form-inline">
      <input type="text"
        name="username"
        class="input-small"
        placeholder="Username" />
      <input type="text" name="message"
        class="input-small"
        placeholder="Message Text" />
      <a id="send" class="btn btn-primary">SEND</a>
    </form>
  </div>
</div>
```

Now we can add the following components to:

- Parse.com collection

- Parse.com model

- Send/add message event

- Getting/displaying messages functions

Backbone-compatible model object/class from Parse.com JS SDK with a mandatory className attribute (this is the name of the collection that will appear in the Data Browser of the Parse.com web interface):

```
Message = Parse.Object.extend({
    className: 'MessageBoard'
})
```

Backbone-compatible collection object from Parse.com JavaScript SDK that points to the model:

```
MessageBoard = Parse.Collection.extend ({
    model: Message
})
```

The home view needs to have the click event listener on the "SEND" button:

```
HomeView = Backbone.View.extend({
    el: '#content',
    template: homeTpl,
    events: {
        'click #send': 'saveMessage'
    },
```

When we create homeView, let's also create a collection and attach event listeners to it:

```
initialize: function() {
    this.collection = new MessageBoard()
    this.collection.bind('all', this.render, this)
    this.collection.fetch()
    this.collection.on('add', function(message) {
        message.save(null, {
            success: function(message) {
                console.log('saved ' + message)
            },
            error: function(message) {
                console.log('error')
            }
        })
        console.log('saved' + message)
    })
},
```

The definition of saveMessage() calls for the "SEND" button click event:

```
saveMessage: function(){
```

Firstly, we get the form object by its ID (#new-message) because it's more effective and readable to use a stored object rather than use jQuery selector every time.

```
var newMessageForm = $('#new-message')
```

The next two lines will get the values of the input fields with names username and message:

```
var username = newMessageForm.find('[name="username"]').val()
var message = newMessageForm.find('[name="message"]').val()
```

Once we have the values of a new message (text and author), we can invoke the `this.collection.add`:

```
this.collection.add({
  'username': username,
  'message': message
})
},
```

Last, we output the collections by using `_.template` with the template and then invoking it with data `this.collection`:

```
render: function() {
    $(this.el).html(_.template(this.template)(this.collection))
}
```

The end result of our manipulations in `app.js` might look something like this:

```
require([
    'libs/text!header.html',
    'libs/text!home.html',
    'libs/text!footer.html'], function (
        headerTpl,
        homeTpl,
        footerTpl) {

    Parse.initialize('your-parse-app-id', 'your-parse-js-sdk-key')

    var ApplicationRouter = Backbone.Router.extend({
        routes: {
            '': 'home',
            '*actions': 'home'
        },
        initialize: function() {
            this.headerView = new HeaderView()
            this.headerView.render()
            this.footerView = new FooterView()
            this.footerView.render()
        },
        home: function() {
            this.homeView = new HomeView()
            this.homeView.render()
        }
    })
})
```

```javascript
HeaderView = Backbone.View.extend ({
    el: '#header',
    templateFileName: 'header.html',
    template: headerTpl,
    initialize: function() {
    },
    render: function() {
        $(this.el).html(_.template(this.template))
    }
})

FooterView = Backbone.View.extend({
    el: '#footer',
    template: footerTpl,
    render: function() {
        this.$el.html(_.template(this.template))
    }
})
Message = Parse.Object.extend({
    className: 'MessageBoard'
})
MessageBoard = Parse.Collection.extend ({
    model: Message
})

HomeView = Backbone.View.extend({
    el: '#content',
    template: homeTpl,
    events: {
        'click #send': 'saveMessage'
    },

    initialize: function(){
        this.collection = new MessageBoard()
        this.collection.bind('all', this.render, this)
        this.collection.fetch()
        this.collection.on('add', function(message) {
            message.save(null, {
                success: function(message) {
                    console.log('saved ' + message)
                },
                error: function(message) {
                    console.log('error')
                }
            })
            console.log('saved' + message)
        })
    },
```

```
        saveMessage: function(){
            var newMessageForm = $('#new-message')
            var username = newMessageForm.find('[name="username"]').val()
            var message = newMessageForm.find('[name="message"]').val()
            this.collection.add({
                'username': username,
                'message': message
                })
        },
        render: function() {
          $(this.el).html(_.template(this.template)(this.collection))
        }
    })

    app = new ApplicationRouter ()
    Backbone.history.start()
})
```

The full source code of the Backbone.js and Parse.com Message Board application is available at https://github.com/azat-co/fullstack-javascript/tree/master/06-board-backbone-parse-sdk.

Taking Message Board Further

Once you are comfortable that your front-end application works well locally, with or without a local HTTP server like MAMP or XAMPP, deploy it to Windows Azure or Heroku. In-depth deployment instructions are described in the "jQuery and Parse.com" chapter.

In the last two examples, Message Board had very basic functionality. You could enhance the application by adding more features.

Additional features for intermediate level developers:

- Sort the list of messages through the *updateAt* attribute before displaying it.

- Add a "Refresh" button to update the list of messages.

- Save the username after the first message entry in a runtime memory or in a session.

- Add an up-vote button next to each message, and store the votes.

- Add a down-vote button next to each message, and store the votes.

Additional features for **advanced** level developers:

- Add a User collection.

- Prevent the same user from voting multiple times.

- Add user sign-up and log-in actions by using Parse.com functions.

- Add a *Delete Message* button next to each message created by a user.

- Add an *Edit Message* button next to each message created by a user.

Summary

This short chapter gives you yet another way of building apps with nothing but JavaScript (and HTML and CSS, obviously). With Parse.com or a similar back-end-as-a-service (BaaS) solution, it is straightforward to persist the data without having to code your own back end. BaaS solutions event takes it a step further by allowing for access-level controls, authentications, server-side logic, and third-party integrations.

In addition to Parse.com, in this chapter we saw how Backbone can be flexible in terms that you can overload its classes to build your own custom ones. This is a way to use Backbone to build your own framework. This is what we did at DocuSign where we had base Backbone models and extended them for custom use cases. We even shared Backbone models between the server and the browser, allowing for faster data loading. Speaking of the server JavaScript, in the next chapter we'll explore how to write JavaScript on the server with Node.js.

■ ■ ■

CHAPTER 6

Intro to Node.js

Any fool can write code that a computer can understand. Good programmers write code that humans can understand.

—Martin Fowler

In this chapter, we'll cover the following:

- Building "Hello World" in Node.js
- Node.js Core Modules
- npm Node Package Manager
- Message Board with Node.js: Memory Store Version
- Unit Testing Node.js

Node.js is a non-blocking platform for building web applications. It uses JavaScript, so it's a centerpiece in our fullstack JavaScript development. We'll start with Hello World and cover core modules and npm. Then, we deploy our Hello World app to cloud.

Building "Hello World" in Node.js

Supplemental video which walks you through the implementation and demonstrates the project: `http://bit.ly/1QnqFmF`.

To check if you have Node.js installed on your computer, type and execute this command in your terminal:

```
$ node -v
```

As of this writing, the latest version is 5.1.0. If you don't have Node.js installed, or if your version is behind, you can download the latest version at `nodejs.org/#download`. You can use one of these tools for version management (i.e., switching between Node.js versions):

- n (`https://github.com/tj/n`)
- nave (`https://github.com/isaacs/nave`)
- nvm (`https://github.com/creationix/nvm`)

As usual, you could copy example code at https://github.com/azat-co/fullstack-javascript/tree/master/07-hello, or write your own program from scratch. If you wish to do the latter, create a folder hello for your "Hello World" Node.js application. Then create file a server.js and line by line type the code below.

This will load the core http module for the server (more on the modules later):

```
var http = require('http')
```

We'll need a port number for our Node.js server. To get it from the environment or assign 1337 if the environment is not set, use:

```
var port = process.env.PORT || 1337
```

This will create a server, and a callback function will contain the response handler code:

```
var server = http.createServer(function (req, res) {
```

To set the right header and status code, use:

```
  res.writeHead(200, {'Content-Type': 'text/plain'})
```

To output "Hello World" with the line end symbol, use:

```
  res.end('Hello World\n')
})
```

To set a port and display the address of the server and the port number, use:

```
server.listen(port, function() {
  console.log('Server is running at %s:%s ',
    server.address().address, server.address().port)
})
```

From the folder in which you have server.js, launch in your terminal the following command:

```
$ node server.js
```

Open localhost:1337 or 127.0.0.1:1337 or any other address you see in the terminal as a result of console.log() function, and you should see "Hello World" in a browser. To shut down the server, press Control + C.

■ **Note** The name of the main file could be different from server.js (e.g., index.js or app.js). In case you need to launch the app.js file, just use $ node app.js.

Node.js Core Modules

Unlike other programming technologies, Node.js doesn't come with a heavy standard library. The core modules of node.js are a bare minimum and the rest can be cherry-picked via the Node Package Manager (NPM) registry. The main core modules, classes, methods, and events include:

- http (`https://nodejs.org/api/http.html#http_http`): Module for working with HTTP protocol

- util (`https://nodejs.org/api/util.html`): Module with various helpers

- querystring (`https://nodejs.org/api/querystring.html`): Module for parsing query string from the URI

- url (`https://nodejs.org/api/url.html`): Module for parsing URI information

- fs (`https://nodejs.org/api/fs.html`): Module for working with the file system

These are the most important core modules. Let's cover each of them.

http

This is the main module responsible for Node.js HTTP server. Here are the main methods:

- `http.createServer()`: returns a new web server object

- `http.listen()`: begins accepting connections on the specified port and hostname

- `http.createClient()`: node app can be a client and make requests to other servers

- `http.ServerRequest()`: incoming requests are passed to request handlers

  - data: emitted when a piece of the message body is received

  - end: emitted exactly once for each request

  - `request.method()`: the request method as a string

  - `request.url()`: request URL string

- `http.ServerResponse()`: this object is created internally by an HTTP server—not by the user, and used as an output of request handlers

  - `response.writeHead()`: sends a response header to the request

  - `response.write()`: sends a response body

  - `response.end()`: sends and ends a response body

util

This module provides utilities for debugging. Some of the methods include:

- `util.inspect()`: Return a string representation of an object, which is useful for debugging

querystring

This module provides utilities for dealing with query strings. Some of the methods include:

- `querystring.stringify()`: Serialize an object to a query string
- `querystring.parse()`: Deserialize a query string to an object

url

This module has utilities for URL resolution and parsing. Some of the methods include:

- `parse()`: Take a URL string, and return an object

fs

fs handles file system operations such as reading and writing to/from files. There are synchronous and asynchronous methods in the library. Some of the methods include:

- `fs.readFile()`: reads file asynchronously
- `fs.writeFile()`: writes data to file asynchronously

There is no need to install or download core modules. To include them in your application, all you need is to follow the syntax:

```
var http = require('http')
```

The lists of non-core modules can be found at:

- npmjs.org: Node Package Manager registry

- Nipster (http://eirikb.github.io/nipster): NPM search tool for Node.js

- node-modules (http://node-modules.com): npm search engine

If you would like to know how to code your own modules, take a look at the article located here: https://quickleft.com/blog/creating-and-publishing-a-node-js-module/.

npm Node Package Manager

Node Package Manager, or NPM, manages dependencies and installs modules for you. Node.js installation comes with NPM, whose web site is npmjs.org.

package.json contains meta information about our Node.js application such as a version number; author name; and, most important, what dependencies we use in the application. All of that information is in the JSON formatted object, which is read by NPM.

If you would like to install packages and dependencies specified in package.json, type:

```
$ npm install
```

A typical package.json file might look like this:

```
{
   "name": "Blerg",
   "description": "Blerg blerg blerg.",
   "version": "0.0.1",
   "author": {
      "name" : "John Doe",
      "email" : "john.doe@gmail.com"
   },
   "repository": {
      "type": "git",
      "url": "http://github.com/johndoe/blerg.git"
   },
   "engines": [
      "node >= 0.6.2"
   ],
   "scripts": {
     "start": "server.js"
   },
```

```
    "license" : "MIT",
    "dependencies": {
        "express": ">= 2.5.6",
        "mustache": "0.4.0",
        "commander": "0.5.2"
    },
    "bin" : {
        "blerg" : "./cli.js"
    }
}
```

While most of the properties in the package.json example above like description and name are self-explanatory, others deserve more explaining. Dependencies is an object, and each item has the name on the left side and the version number on the right side (e.g., "express": ">= 2.5.6"). The version can be exact: for example, "express": "2.5.6," or greater than, or wild-card, for example, "express": "*" (a great way to blow up your app in production with new untested dependencies: therefore not recommended).

The bin property is for command-line utilities. It tells the system what file to launch. And the scripts object has scripts that you can launch with $ npm run SCRIPT_NAME. The start script and test are exceptions. You can run them with $ npm start and $ npm test.

To update a package to its current latest version or the latest version that is allowable by the version specification defined in package.json, use:

```
$ npm update name-of-the-package
```

Or for single module installation:

```
$ npm install name-of-the-package
```

The only module used in this book's examples—and which does not belong to the core Node.js package—is mongodb. We'll install it later in the book.

Heroku will need package.json to run NPM on the server.

For more information on NPM, take a look at the article "Tour of NPM" (http://tobyho.com/2012/02/09/tour-of-npm).

Deploying "Hello World" to PaaS

For Heroku and Windows Azure deployment, we'll need a Git repository. To create it from the root of your project, type the following command in your terminal:

```
$ git init
```

Git will create a hidden .git folder. Now we can add files and make the first commit:

```
$ git add .
$ git commit -am "first commit"
```

■ **Tip** To view hidden files on the Mac OS X Finder app, execute this command in a terminal window: `defaults write com.apple.finder AppleShowAllFiles -bool true`. To change the flag back to hidden: `defaults write com.apple.finder AppleShowAllFiles -bool false`.

Deploying to Windows Azure

In order to deploy our "Hello World" application to Windows Azure, we must add Git **remote**. You could copy the URL from Windows Azure Portal, under Web Site, and use it with this command:

```
$ git remote add azure yourURL
```

Now we should be able to make a push with this command:

```
$ git push azure master
```

If everything went okay, you should see success logs in the terminal and "Hello World" in the browser of your Windows Azure Web Site URL.

To push changes, just execute:

```
$ git add .
$ git commit -m "changing to hello azure"
$ git push azure master
```

A more meticulous guide can be found in the tutorial https://azure.microsoft.com/en-us/documentation/articles/web-sites-nodejs-develop-deploy-mac.

Deploying to Heroku

For Heroku deployment, we need to create two extra files: `Procfile` and `package.json`. You could get the source code from https://github.com/azat-co/fullstack-javascript/tree/master/07-hello or write your own one.

The structure of the "Hello World" application looks like this:

```
/07-hello
  -package.json
  -Procfile
  -server.js
```

Procfile is a mechanism for declaring what commands are run by your application's dynos on the Heroku platform. Basically, it tells Heroku what processes to run. Procfile has only one line in this case:

```
web: node server.js
```

For this example, we keep package.json simple:

```
{
  "name": "node-example",
  "version": "0.0.1",
  "dependencies": {
  },
  "engines": {
    "node": ">=0.6.x"
  }
}
```

After we have all of the files in the project folder, we can use Git to deploy the application. The commands are pretty much the same as with Windows Azure except that we need to add Git remote, and create Cedar stack with:

```
$ heroku create
```

After it's done, we push and update with:

```
$ git push heroku master
$ git add .
$ git commit -am "changes :+1:"
$ git push heroku master
```

If everything went okay, you should see success logs in the terminal and "Hello World" in the browser of your Heroku app URL.

Message Board with Node.js: Memory Store Version

Supplemental video which walks you through the implementation and demonstrates the project: http://bit.ly/1Qnq09P.

The first version of the Message Board back-end application will store messages only in runtime memory storage for the sake of KISS (http://en.wikipedia.org/wiki/KISS_principle). That means that each time we start/reset the server, the data will be lost.

We'll start with a simple test case first to illustrate the Test-Driven Development approach. The full code is available at https://github.com/azat-co/fullstack-javascript/tree/master/08-test.

Unit Testing Node.js

We should have two methods:

1. Get all of the messages as an array of JSON objects for the GET /message endpoint using the getMessages() method

2. Add a new message with properties name and message for POST /messages route via the addMessage() function

We'll start by creating an empty mb-server.js file. After it's there, let's switch to tests and create the test.js file with the following content:

```
var http = require('http')
var assert = require('assert')
var querystring = require('querystring')
var util = require('util')

var messageBoard = require('./mb-server')

assert.deepEqual('[{"name":"John","message":"hi"}]',
  messageBoard.getMessages())
assert.deepEqual ('{"name":"Jake","message":"gogo"}',
  messageBoard.addMessage ("name=Jake&message=gogo"))
assert.deepEqual('[{"name":"John","message":"hi"},{"name":"Jake",
message":"gogo"}]',
  messageBoard.getMessages())
```

Please keep in mind that this is a very simplified comparison of strings and not JavaScript objects. So every space, quote, and case matters. You could make the comparison "smarter" by parsing a string into a JSON object with:

```
JSON.parse(str)
```

For testing our assumptions, we use core the Node.js module assert. It provides a bunch of useful methods like equal(), deepEqual(), etc.

More advanced libraries include alternative interfaces with TDD and/or BDD approaches:

- Expect: Minimalistic BDD-style assertion library:, for example, expect(user.name).to.eql('azat')

- Should (https://github.com/shouldjs/should.js): BDD-style assertion library that works by modifying Object.prototype: for example, user.name.should.be.eql('azat')

For more Test-Driven Development and cutting-edge automated testing, you could use the following libraries and modules:

- Mocha (https://mochajs.org/): Feature-rich testing framework (my default choice)

- NodeUnit (https://github.com/caolan/nodeunit): Simple assert-style unit testing library

- Jasmine (https://github.com/jasmine/jasmine): BDD testing framework with built-in assertion and spy (for mocking) libraries

- Vows (http://vowsjs.org/): BDD framework for Node.js tailored to testing asynchronous code

- Chai (http://chaijs.com/): BDD/TDD assertion library that can be paired with a testing framework and has its own versions of Should, Expect, and Assert

- Tape (https://github.com/substack/tape): A minimalistic TAP (Test Anything Protocol) library

- Jest (http://facebook.github.io/jest/): Jasmine-and-Expect-like testing library with automatic mocks

You could copy the "Hello World" script into the mb-server.js file for now or even keep it empty. If we run test.js by the terminal command:

```
$ node test.js
```

We should see an error. Probably something like this one:

```
TypeError: Object #<Object> has no method 'getMessages'
```

That's totally fine, because we haven't written getMessages() method yet. So let's do it and make our application more useful by adding two new methods: to get the list of the messages for Chat and to add a new message to the collection.

mb-server.js file with global exports object:

```
exports.getMessages = function() {
  return JSON.stringify(messages)
  // Output array of messages as a string/text
}
exports.addMessage = function (data){
  messages.push(querystring.parse(data))
  // To convert string into JavaScript object we use parse/deserializer
  return JSON.stringify(querystring.parse(data))
  // Output new message in JSON as a string
}
```

We import dependencies:

```
var http = require('http')
// Loads http module
var util= require('util')
// Usefull functions
var querystring = require('querystring')
// Loads querystring module, we'll need it to serialize and deserialize
objects and query strings
```

And set the port. If it's set in the env var, we use that value; and if it's not set, we use a hard-coded value of 1337:

```
var port = process.env.PORT || 1337
```

So far, nothing fancy, right? To store the list of messages, we'll use an array:

```
var messages=[]
// This array will hold our messages
messages.push({
  'name': 'John',
  'message': 'hi'
})
// Sample message to test list method
```

Generally, fixtures like dummy data belong to the test/spec files and not to the main application code base.

Our server code will look slightly more interesting. For getting the list of messages, according to REST methodology, we need to make a GET request. For creating/adding a new message, it should be a POST request. So in our createServer object, we should add req.method() and req.url() to check for an HTTP request type and a URL path.

Let's load the http module:

```
var http = require('http')
```

We'll need some of the handy functions from the util and querystring modules (to serialize and deserialize objects and query strings):

```
var util= require('util')
// Usefull functions
var querystring = require('querystring')
// Loads querystring module, we'll need it to serialize and deserialize
objects and query strings
```

To create a server and expose it to outside modules (i.e., test.js):

```
exports.server=http.createServer(function (req, res) {
// Creates server
```

Inside of the request handler callback, we should check if the request method is POST and the URL is messages/create.json:

```
if (req.method == 'POST' && req.url == '/messages/create.json') {
  // If method is POST and URL is messages/ add message to the array
```

If the condition above is true, we add a message to the array. However, data must be converted to a string type (with encoding UTF-8) prior to the adding, because it is a type of Buffer:

```
var message = ''
req.on('data', function(data, msg){
  console.log(data.toString('utf-8'))
  message=exports.addMessage(data.toString('utf-8'))
  // Data is type of Buffer and must be converted to string with
  encoding UTF-8 first
  // Adds message to the array
})
```

These logs will help us to monitor the server activity in the terminal:

```
req.on('end', function(){
  console.log('message', util.inspect(message, true, null))
  console.log('messages:', util.inspect(messages, true, null))
  // Debugging output into the terminal
```

The output should be in a text format with a status of 200 (okay):

```
  res.writeHead(200, {'Content-Type': 'text/plain'})
  // Sets the right header and status code
```

We output a message with a newly created object ID:

```
  res.end(message)
  // Out put message, should add object id
})
```

If the method is GET and the URL is /messages/list.json output a list of messages:

```
} else
if (req.method == 'GET' && req.url == '/messages/list.json') {
// If method is GET and URL is /messages output list of messages
```

Fetch a list of messages:

```
var body = exports.getMessages()
// Body will hold our output
```

The response body will hold our output:

```
res.writeHead(200, {
  'Content-Length': body.length,
  'Content-Type': 'text/plain'
})
res.end(body)
```

The next else is for when there's not matches for any of the previous conditions. This sets the right header and status code:

```
} else {
  res.writeHead(200, {'Content-Type': 'text/plain'})
  // Sets the right header and status code
```

In case it's neither of the two endpoints above, we output a string with a line end symbol:

```
res.end('Hello World\n')
// Outputs string with line end symbol
}
```

Start the server:

```
}).listen(port)
// Sets port and IP address of the server
```

Now, we should set a port and IP address of the server:

```
console.log('Server running at http://127.0.0.1:%s/', port)
```

We expose methods for the unit testing in test.js (exports keyword), and this function returns an array of messages as a string/text:

```
exports.getMessages = function() {
  return JSON.stringify(messages)
}
```

addMessage() converts a string into a JavaScript object with the parse/deserializer method from querystring:

```
exports.addMessage = function (data){
  messages.push(querystring.parse(data))
```

Also returning a new message in a JSON-as-a-string format:

```
  return JSON.stringify(querystring.parse(data))
}
```

Here is the full code of mb-server.js minus the comments. It's also available at 08-test:

```
var http = require('http')
// Loads http module
var util= require('util')
// Usefull functions
var querystring = require('querystring')
// Loads querystring module, we'll need it to serialize and deserialize
objects and query strings

var port = process.env.PORT || 1337

var messages=[]
// This array will hold our messages
messages.push({
  'name': 'John',
  'message': 'hi'
})
// Sample message to test list method

exports.server=http.createServer(function (req, res) {
// Creates server
  if (req.method == 'POST' && req.url == '/messages/create.json') {
    // If method is POST and URL is messages/ add message to the array
    var message = ''
    req.on('data', function(data, msg){
      console.log(data.toString('utf-8'))
      message=exports.addMessage(data.toString('utf-8'))
      // Data is type of Buffer and must be converted to string with
      encoding UTF-8 first
      // Adds message to the array
    })
    req.on('end', function(){
      console.log('message', util.inspect(message, true, null))
      console.log('messages:', util.inspect(messages, true, null))
      // Debugging output into the terminal
      res.writeHead(200, {'Content-Type': 'text/plain'})
      // Sets the right header and status code
      res.end(message)
      // Out put message, should add object id
    })
  } else
```

```
  if (req.method == 'GET' && req.url == '/messages/list.json') {
  // If method is GET and URL is /messages output list of messages
    var body = exports.getMessages()
    // Body will hold our output
    res.writeHead(200, {
      'Content-Length': body.length,
      'Content-Type': 'text/plain'
    })
    res.end(body)
  } else {
    res.writeHead(200, {'Content-Type': 'text/plain'})
    // Sets the right header and status code
    res.end('Hello World\n')
    // Outputs string with line end symbol
  }

}).listen(port)
// Sets port and IP address of the server
console.log('Server running at http://127.0.0.1:%s/', port)


exports.getMessages = function() {
  return JSON.stringify(messages)
  // Output array of messages as a string/text
}
exports.addMessage = function (data){
  messages.push(querystring.parse(data))
  // To convert string into JavaScript object we use parse/deserializer
  return JSON.stringify(querystring.parse(data))
  // Output new message in JSON as a string
}
```

To check it, go to localhost:1337/messages/list.json. You should see an example message.

Alternatively, you could use the terminal command to fetch the messages:

```
$ curl http://127.0.0.1:1337/messages/list.json
```

To make the POST request by using a command-line interface:

```
$ curl -d "name=BOB&message=test" http://127.0.0.1:1337/messages/create.json
```

And you should get the output in a server terminal window and a new message "test" when you refresh localhost:1337/messages/list.json. Needless to say, all three tests should pass.

Your application might grow bigger with more methods, URL paths to parse and conditions. That is where frameworks come in handy. They provide helpers to process requests and other nice things like static file support, sessions, etc. In this example, we intentionally didn't use any frameworks like Express (http://expressjs.com/) or Restify (http://mcavage.github.com/node-restify/). Other notable Node.js frameworks:

- Derby (http://derbyjs.com/):MVC framework making it easy to write real-time, collaborative applications that run in both Node.js and browsers

- Express.js (http://expressjs.com/en/index.html): the most robust, tested and used Node.js framework

- Restify (http://restify.com/): lightweight framework for REST API servers

- Sails.js (http://sailsjs.org/): MVC Node.js framework

- hapi (http://spumko.github.io/): Node.js framework built on top of Express.js

- Connect (https://github.com/senchalabs/connect#readme): a middleware framework for node, shipping with over 18 bundled middlewares and a rich selection of third-party middleware

- GeddyJS (http://geddyjs.org/): a simple, structured MVC web framework for Node

- CompoundJS (http://compoundjs.com/) (ex-RailswayJS): Node.JS MVC framework based on ExpressJS

- Tower.js (http://tower.github.io/): a full stack web framework for Node.js and the browser

- Meteor (https://www.meteor.com/): open-source platform for building top-quality web apps in a fraction of the time

For a list of hand-picked frameworks, take a look at (http://nodeframeworks.com). Ways to improve the application:

- Improve existing test cases by adding object comparison instead of a string one

- Move the seed data to test.js from mb-server.js

- Add test cases to support your front-end (e.g., up-vote, user log in)

- Add methods to support your front-end (e.g., up-vote, user log in)

- Generate unique IDs for each message and store them in a Hash instead of an Array

- Install Mocha and re-factor test.js so it uses this library

So far we've been storing our messages in the application memory, so each time the application is restarted, we lose it. To fix it, we need to add a persistence, and one of the ways is to use a database like MongoDB.

Summary

In this chapter we've covered important topics that will lay the foundation. They exhibit the "Hello World" application in Node.js, list of some of its most important core modules, NPM workflow, detailed commands for deployment of Node.js apps to Heroku and Windows Azure; and an example of a test-driven development practice.

CHAPTER 7

■ ■ ■

Intro to MongoDB

What is Oracle? A bunch of people. And all of our products were just ideas in the heads of those people - ideas that people typed into a computer, tested, and that turned out to be the best idea for a database or for a programming language.

—Larry Ellison

In this chapter, we'll explore the following topics:

- MongoDB Shell

- MongoDB Native Driver for Node.js

- MongoDB on Heroku with MongoLab

- Message Board: MongoDB Version

MongoDB is a NoSQL document-store database. It is scalable and performant. It has no schema so all the logic and relationships are implemented in the application layer. You can use ODMs like Waterline or Mongoose for that. MongoDB uses JavaScript interface, which completes the full stack JavaScript stack puzzle of browser, server, and the database layers. With MongoDB we can use one language for all three layers. The easiest way to get started with MongoDB is to use its shell, a.k.a. REPL (read-eval-print-loop).

MongoDB Shell

If you haven't done so already, please install the latest version of MongoDB from mongodb.org/downloads. For more instructions, please refer to the Database:MongoDB section in Chapter 2. You might have to create a data folder per instructions.

Now from the folder where you unpacked the archive, launch the mongod service with:

```
$ ./bin/mongod
```

You should be able to see information in your terminal and in the browser at localhost:28017.

For the MongoDB shell, or mongo, launch in a new terminal window (**important!**), and at the same folder this command:

```
$ ./bin/mongo
```

You should see something like this, depending on your version of the MongoDB shell:

```
MongoDB shell version: 2.0.6
connecting to: test
```

To test the database, use the JavaScript-like interface and commands save and find:

```
> db.test.save( { a: 1 } )
> db.test.find()
```

More detailed step-by-step instructions are available in the Database:MongoDB section of Chapter 2.

Some other useful MongoDB shell commands from MongoDB and Mongoose cheatsheet (https://gum.co/mongodb/git-874e6fb4):

- > show dbs: show databases on the server

- > use DB_NAME: select database DB_NAME

- > show collections: show collections in the selected database

- > db.COLLECTION_NAME.find(): perform the find query on collection with the COLLECTION_NAME name to find any items

- > db.COLLECTION_NAME.find({"_id": ObjectId("549d9a30 81d0f07866fdaac6")}): perform the find query on collection with the COLLECTION_NAME name to find item with ID 549d9a3081d0f07866fdaac6

- > db.COLLECTION_NAME.find({"email": /gmail/}): perform the find query on collection with the COLLECTION_NAME name to find items with e-mail property matching /gmail

- > db.COLLECTION_NAME.update(QUERY_OBJECT, SET_OBJECT): perform the update query on collection with the COLLECTION_NAME name to update items that match QUERY_OBJECT with SET_OBJECT

- > db.COLLECTION_NAME.remove(QUERY_OBJECT): perform remove query for items matching QUERY_OBJECT criteria on the COLLECTION_NAME collection

- > db.COLLECTION_NAME.insert(OBJECT): add OBJECT to the collection with the COLLECTION_NAME name

So starting from a fresh shell session, you can execute these commands to create a document, change it, and remove:

```
> help
> show dbs
> use board
> show collections
> db.messages.remove();
> var a = db.messages.findOne();
> printjson(a);
> a.message = "hi";
> a.name = "John";
> db.messages.save(a);
> db.messages.find({});
> db.messages.update({name: "John"},{$set: {message: "bye"}});
> db.messages.find({name: "John"});
> db.messages.remove({name: "John"});
```

You can download the MongoDB and Mongoose cheatsheet as a PDF (https://gumroad.com/l/mongodb/fsjs-CB07C579#) or view it online at https://github.com/mongodb/node-mongodb-native/#data-types.

A full overview of the MongoDB interactive shell is available at mongodb.org: Overview – The MongoDB Interactive Shell (https://docs.mongodb.org/manual/tutorial/getting-started-with-the-mongo-shell/).

BSON

Binary JSON, or BSON, is a special data type that MongoDB utilizes. It is like JSON in notation but has support for additional more sophisticated data types such as buffer or date.

A word of caution about BSON: ObjectId in MongoDB is an equivalent to ObjectID in MongoDB Native Node.js Driver (i.e., make sure to use the proper case). Otherwise you'll get an error. More on the types: ObjectId in MongoDB (http://www.mongodb.org/display/DOCS/Object+IDs) vs Data Types in MongoDB Native Node.js Drier (https://github.com/mongodb/node-mongodb-native/#data-types). Example of Node.js code with mongodb.ObjectID(): collection.findOne({_id: new ObjectID(idString)}, console.log) // ok. On the other hand, in the MongoDB shell, we employ: db.messages.findOne({_id:ObjectId(idStr)});.

MongoDB Native Driver

Supplemental video which walks you through the implementation and demonstrates the project: http://bit.ly/1QnqZSk.

We'll use Node.js Native Driver for MongoDB (https://github.com/christkv/node-mongodb-native) to access MongoDB from Node.js applications. Full documentation is also available at http://mongodb.github.com/node-mongodb-native/api-generated/db.html.

To install MongoDB Native driver for Node.js, use:

```
$ npm install mongodb
```

More details are at http://www.mongodb.org/display/DOCS/node.JS.
Don't forget to include the dependency in the package.json file as well:

```
{
  "name": "node-example",
  "version": "0.0.1",
  "dependencies": {
    "mongodb":"",
    ...
  },
  "engines": {
    "node": ">=0.6.x"
  }
}
```

Alternatively, for your own development you could use other mappers, which are available as an extension of the Native Driver:

- Mongoskin (https://github.com/guileen/node-mongoskin): a future layer for node-mongodb-native

- Mongoose (http://mongoosejs.com/): an asynchronous JavaScript driver with optional support for modeling

- Mongolia (https://github.com/masylum/mongolia): a lightweight MongoDB ORM/driver wrapper

- Monk (https://github.com/Automattic/monk): a tiny layer that provides simple yet substantial usability improvements for MongoDB usage within Node.js

This small example will test if we can connect to local MongoDB instance from a Node.js script.

After we install the library, we can include the mongodb library in our app.js file:

```
var util = require('util')
var mongodb = require ('mongodb')
```

This is one of the ways to establish connection to the MongoDB server in which the db variable will hold reference to the database at a specified host and port:

```
var Db = mongodb.Db
var Connection = mongodb.Connection
var Server = mongodb.Server
var host = '127.0.0.1'
var port = 27017

var db=new Db ('test', new Server(host,port, {}))
```

To actually open a connection:

```
db.open(function(error, connection){
  // Do something with the database here
  db.close()
})
```

To check that we have the connection, we need to handle error. Also, let's get the admin object with db.admin() and fetch the list of databases with listDatabases():

```
var db=new Db ('test', new Server(host, port, {}))
db.open(function(error, connection){
    console.log('error: ', error)
    var adminDb = db.admin()
    adminDb.listDatabases(function(error, dbs) {
    console.log('error: ', error)
        console.log('databases: ', dbs.databases)
    db.close()
  })
})
```

This code snippet is available at https://github.com/mongodb/node-mongodb-native/#data-types. If we run it, it should output "connected" in the terminal. When you're in doubt and need to check the properties of an object, there is a useful method in the util module:

```
console.log(util.inspect(db))
```

Now you might want to set up the database in the cloud and test the connection from your Node.js script.

MongoDB on Heroku: MongoLab

Supplemental video which walks you through the implementation and demonstrates the project: http://bit.ly/1Qnr8Fn.

After you made your application that displays 'connected' work locally, it's time to slightly modify it and deploy to the platform as a service (i.e., Heroku).

We recommend using the MongoLab add-on (https://elements.heroku.com/addons/mongolab). MongoLab add-on provides a browser-based GUI to look up and manipulate the data and collections. More information is available at https://elements.heroku.com/addons/mongolab#docs.

■ **Note**   You might have to provide your credit card information to use MongoLab even if you select the free version. You should not be charged, though.

In order to connect to the database server, there is a database connection URL (a.k.a. MongoLab URL/URI), which is a way to transfer all of the necessary information to make a connection to the database in one string.

The database connection string MONGOLAB_URI has the following format:

```
mongodb://user:pass@server_NAME.mongolab.com:PORT/db_name
```

You could either copy the MongoLab URL string from the Heroku web site (and hard-code it) or get the string from the Node.js process.env object:

```
process.env.MONGOLAB_URI
```

or

```
var connectionUri = url.parse(process.env.MONGOLAB_URI)
```

The global object process gives access to environment variables via process.env. Those variables conventionally used to pass database host names and ports, passwords, API keys, port numbers, and other system information that shouldn't be hard-coded into the main logic.

To make our code work both locally and on Heroku, we can use the logical OR operator || and assign a local host and port if environment variables are undefined:

```
var port = process.env.PORT || 1337
var dbConnUrl = process.env.MONGOLAB_URI ||
  'mongodb://127.0.0.1:27017/test'
```

Here is our updated cross-environment ready app.js file (https://github.com/azat-co/fullstack-javascript/tree/master/10-db-connect-heroku). I added a method to get the list of collections listCollections instead of getting the list of the databases (we have only one database in MongoLab right now):

```
var util = require('util')
var url = require('url')
var client = require ('mongodb').MongoClient

var dbConnUrl = process.env.MONGOLAB_URI ||
  'mongodb://127.0.0.1:27017/test'

console.log('db server: ', dbConnUrl)

client.connect(dbConnUrl, {}, function(error, db){
    console.log('error: ', error)
    db.listCollections().toArray(function(err, collections) {
    console.log('error: ', error)
        console.log('collections: ', collections)
    db.close()
    })
})
```

Following the modification of app.js by addition of MONGOLAB_URI, we can now initialize Git repository, create a Heroku app, add the MongoLab add-on to it, and deploy the app with Git.

Utilize the same steps as in the previous examples to create a new git repository:

```
$ git init
$ git add .
$ git commit -am 'initial commit'
```

Create the Cedar stack Heroku app:

```
$ heroku create
```

If everything went well you should be able to see a message that tell you the new Heroku app name (and URL) along with a message that remote was added. Having remote in your local git is crucial; you can always check a list of remote by:

```
$ git remote show
```

To install free MongoLab on the existing Heroku app (add-ons work on a per app basis), use:

```
$ heroku addons:create mongolab:sandbox
```

Or log on to Heroku (https://elements.heroku.com/addons/mongolab) with your Heroku credentials and choose MongoLab Free for that particular Heroku app, if you know the name of that app.

The project folder needs to have Procfile and package.json. You can copy them from https://github.com/azat-co/fullstack-javascript/tree/master/10-db-connect-heroku.

Now you can push you code to Heroku with:

```
$ git push heroku master
```

Enjoy the the log that should tell you that the deploy was successful. Now see the output with this command:

```
$ heroku logs
```

The result will be something like this:

```
2015-12-01T12:34:51.438633+00:00 app[web.1]: db server:
mongodb://heroku_cxgh54g6:9d76gspc45v899i44sm6bn790c@ds035617.mongolab.com:
34457/heroku_cxgh54g6
2015-12-01T12:34:53.264530+00:00 app[web.1]: error:  null
2015-12-01T12:34:53.236398+00:00 app[web.1]: error:  null
```

```
2015-12-01T12:34:53.271775+00:00 app[web.1]: collections:  [ { name:
'system.indexes', options: {} },
2015-12-01T12:34:53.271778+00:00 app[web.1]:    { name: 'test', options: {
autoIndexId: true } } ]
```

If you get app.js and modified app.js files working, let's enhance by adding a HTTP server, so the 'connected' message will be displayed in the browser instead of the terminal window. To do so, we'll wrap the server object instantiation in a database connection callback (file 11-db-server/app.js at https://github.com/azat-co/fullstack-javascript/blob/master/11-db/app.js).

Supplemental video which walks you through the implementation and demonstrates the project:

```
http://bit.ly/1Qnrmwr.
var util = require('util')
var url = require('url')
var http = require('http')
var mongodb = require ('mongodb')
var client = require ('mongodb').MongoClient

var port = process.env.PORT || 1337
var dbConnUrl = process.env.MONGOLAB_URI || 'mongodb://@127.0.0.1:27017/test'

client.connect(dbConnUrl, {}, function(error, db) {
    console.log('error: ', error)
    db.listCollections().toArray(function(error, collections) {
    console.log('error: ', error)
        console.log('collections: ', collections)
        var server = http.createServer(function (request, response) {
        // Creates server
          response.writeHead(200, {'Content-Type': 'text/plain'})
          // Sets the right header and status code
          response.end(util.inspect(collections))  // Outputs string with
          line end symbol
        })
        server.listen(port, function() {
            console.log('Server is running at %s:%s ', server.address().
            address, server.address().port) // Sets port and IP address of
            the server
        })
    db.close()
    })
})
```

The final Heroku-deployment-ready project is located at https://github.com/azat-co/fullstack-javascript/tree/master/11-db-serverunder.

After the deployment you should be able to open the URL provided by Heroku and see the list of collections. If it's a newly created app with an empty database, there would be no collections. You can create a collection using the MongoLab web interface in Heroku.

For more information on the native MongoDB driver, check out http://mongodb. github.io/node-mongodb-native/api-articles/nodekoarticle1.html

Message Board: MongoDB Version

Supplemental video which walks you through the implementation and demonstrates the project: http://bit.ly/1QnsfoE.

We should have everything set up for writing the Node.js application that will work both locally and on Heroku. The source code is available at https://github.com/azat-co/fullstack-javascript/tree/master/12-board-api-mongonder. The structure of the application is simple:

```
/12-board-api-mongo
  -web.js
  -Procfile
  -package.json
```

This is what web.js looks like; first we include our libraries:

```
var http = require('http')
var util = require('util')
var querystring = require('querystring')
var client = require('mongodb').MongoClient
```

Then put out a magic string to connect to MongoDB:

```
var uri = process.env.MONGOLAB_URI || 'mongodb://@127.0.0.1:27017/messages'
```

■ **Note** The URI/URL format contains the optional database name in which our collection will be stored. Feel free to change it to something else: for example, 'rpjs' or 'test'.

We put all the logic inside of an open connection in the form of a callback function:

```
client.connect(uri, function(error, db) {
  if (error) return console.error(error)
```

We are getting the collection with the next statement:

```
var collection = db.collection('messages')
```

Now we can instantiate the server and set up logic to process our endpoints/routes. We need to fetch the documents on GET /messages/list.json:

```
var app = http.createServer( function (request, response) {
    if (request.method === 'GET' && request.url ===
    '/messages/list.json') {
        collection.find().toArray(function(error,results) {
            response.writeHead(200,{ 'Content-Type': 'text/plain'})
            console.dir(results)
            response.end(JSON.stringify(results))
        })
```

On the POST /messages/create.json, we inserting the document:

```
    } else if (request.method === 'POST' && request.url ===
    '/messages/create.json') {
        request.on('data', function(data) {
            collection.insert(querystring.parse(data.toString('utf-8')),
            {safe:true}, function(error, obj) {
                if (error) throw error
                response.end(JSON.stringify(obj))
            })
        })
    } else {
```

This will be shown in the event that the client request is not matching any of the conditions above. This is a good reminder for us when we try to go to the http://localhost:1337 instead of http://localhost:1337/messages/list.json:

```
        response.end('Supported endpoints: \n/messages/list.json\n/
        messages/create.json')
    }
})
var port = process.env.PORT || 1337
app.listen(port)
})
```

■ **Note** We don't have to use additional words after the collection/entity name; that is, instead of /messages/list.json and /messages/create.json it's perfectly fine to have just /messages for all the HTTP methods such as GET, POST, PUT, DELETE. If you change them in your application code make sure to use the updated CURL commands and front-end code.

To test via CURL terminal commands run:

```
$ curl http://localhost:5000/messages/list.json
```

Or open your browser at the `http://locahost:1337/messages/list.json` location. It should give you an empty array: [ ], which is fine. Then POST a new message:

```
$ curl  -d "username=BOB&message=test" http://localhost:5000/messages/
create.json
```

Now we must see a response containing an ObjectID of a newly created element, for example: [{"username":"BOB","message":"test","_id":"51edc ad45862430000000001"}]. Your ObjectId might vary.

If everything works as it should locally, try to deploy it to Heroku.

To test the application on Heroku, you could use the same CURL commands (`http://curl.haxx.se/docs/manpage.html`), substituting `http://localhost/` or "`http://127.0.0.1`" with your unique Heroku app's host/URL:

```
$ curl http://your-app-name.herokuapp.com/messages/list.json
$ curl -d "username=BOB&message=test"
  http://your-app-name.herokuapp.com/messages/create.json
```

It's also nice to double check the database either via Mongo shell: `$ mongo` terminal command and then `use twitter-clone` and `db.messages.find()`; or via MongoHub (`https://github.com/bububa/MongoHub-Mac`), mongoui (`https://github.com/azat-co/mongoui`), mongo-express(`https://github.com/andzdroid/mongo-express`) or in case of MongoLab through its web interface accessible at the heroku.com web site.

If you would like to use another domain name instead of `http://your-app-name.herokuapp.com`, you'll need to do two things:

1. Tell Heroku your domain name:

   ```
   $ heroku domains:add www.your-domain-name.com
   ```

2. Add the CNAME DNS record in your DNS manager to point to `http://your-app-name.herokuapp.com`.

More information on custom domains can be found at `devcenter.heroku.com/articles/custom-domains`

■ **Tip**   For more productive and efficient development we should automate as much as possible; that is, use tests instead of CURL commands. There is an article on the Mocha library in the BONUS chapter that, along with the `superagent` or `request` libraries, is a timesaver for such tasks.

Summary

In this chapter we've covered the MongoDB database and its shell. MongoDB uses an extended version of JSON, which is called BSON. Then we switched to Node.js with the native MongoDB driver. Many other MongoDB Node.js libraries depend on the native driver and build on top of it. For this reason, it's good to know it. To use MongoDB on Heroku, we utilized MongoLab add-on (the magical `MONGOLAB_URI`). Finally, we use the acquired knowledge to add persistence to the Message Boards application.

CHAPTER 8

■ ■ ■

Putting It All Together

Debugging is twice as hard as writing the code in the first place. Therefore, if you write the code as cleverly as possible, you are, by definition, not smart enough to debug it.

—Brian W. Kernighan

In this chapter, we'll cover:

- Adding CORS for Different Domain Deployment

- Message Board UI

- Message Board API

- Deployment to Heroku

- Same Domain Deployment Server

- Deployment to Amazon Web Services

Now, it would be good if we could put our front-end and back-end applications so they could work together. There are a few ways to do it:

- Different domains (Heroku apps) for front-end and back-end apps: make sure there are no cross-domain issues by using CORS or JSONP. This approach is covered in detail later.

- Same domain deployment: make sure Node.js process static resources and assets for front-end application—not recommended for serious production applications.

Adding CORS for Different Domain Deployment

This is, so far, the best practice for the production environment. Back-end applications are usually deployed at the `http://app.` or `http://api.` subdomains.

One way to make a different domain deployment work is to overcome the same-domain limitation of AJAX technology with JSONP:

```
var request = $.ajax({
  url: url,
  dataType: 'jsonp',
  data: {...},
  jsonpCallback: 'fetchData,
  type: 'GET'
})
```

The other, and better, way to do it is to add the OPTIONS method, and special headers, which are called cross-origin resource sharing or CORS (https://en.wikipedia.org/wiki/Cross-origin_resource_sharing), to the Node.js server app before the output:

```
...
response.writeHead(200,{
  'Access-Control-Allow-Origin': origin,
  'Content-Type':'text/plain',
  'Content-Length':body.length
})
...
```

or

```
...
res.writeHead(200, {
  'Access-Control-Allow-Origin', 'your-domain-name',
  ...
})
...
```

The need for the OPTIONS method is outlined in HTTP access control (https://developer.mozilla.org/en-US/docs/Web/HTTP/Access_control_CORS). The OPTIONS request can be dealt with in the following manner:

```
...
if (request.method=="OPTIONS") {
  response.writeHead("204", "No Content", {
    "Access-Control-Allow-Origin": origin,
    "Access-Control-Allow-Methods":
      "GET, POST, PUT, DELETE, OPTIONS",
```

```
    "Access-Control-Allow-Headers": "content-type, accept",
    "Access-Control-Max-Age": 10, // Seconds.
    "Content-Length": 0
  })
  response.end();
};
...
```

Message Board UI

Supplemental video which walks you through the implementation and demonstrates the project: http://bit.ly/1QnsvEb.

Our front-end application used Parse.com as a replacement for a back-end application. Now we can switch to our own back end replacing the endpoints along with a few other painless changes. Let me walk you through them.

In the beginning of the app.js file, uncomment the first line for running locally, or replace the URL values with your Heroku or Windows Azure back-end application public URLs:

```
// var URL = 'http://localhost:1337/'
var URL ='http://your-app-name.herokuapp.com/'
```

Most of the code in app.js and the folder structure remained intact from the 06-board-backbone-parse-sdk project, with the exception of replacing Parse.com models and collections with original Backbone.js ones. So go ahead and type or copy the RequireJS block for loading of the dependencies (templates in this case):

```
require([
    'libs/text!header.html',
    'libs/text!home.html',
    'libs/text!footer.html'],
    function (
        headerTpl,
        homeTpl,
        footerTpl) {
```

The ApplicationRouter, HeaderView, and FooterView are the same as in the 06-board-backbone-parse-sdk project so I won't list them here again.

We need to change the the model and collection to this from using `Parse.Object` and `Parse.Collection`. Those are the places where Backbone.js looks up for REST API URLs corresponding to the specific collection and model:

```
Message = Backbone.Model.extend({
    url: URL + 'messages/create.json'
})
MessageBoard = Backbone.Collection.extend ({
    model: Message,
    url: URL + 'messages/list.json'
})
```

Next is the `HomeView` where most of the logic resides. I made a few enhancements to the rendering process, which is a good illustration of what you can do with events in Backbone. First, create the view and define the element selector, template (loaded via RequireJS and text plug-in), and event for the SEND button:

```
HomeView = Backbone.View.extend({
    el: '#content',
    template: homeTpl,
    events: {
        'click #send': 'saveMessage'
    },
```

Now, in the constructor of the view set the `homeView` to `this` so we can use `this` later by the name inside of the closures (otherwise, `this` can mutate inside of the closures):

```
initialize: function() {
    var homeView = this
```

Then, I attached an event listener `refresh` that will do the rendering. Prior to that we had the `all` event, which wasn't very good, because it triggered re-rendering the addition of each message. You see, `fetch` will trigger `add` as many times as there are messages (10, 100, 1000, etc.) and if we use `all` event listener, `add` is part of `all`. While with this custom event `refresh` we can trigger rendering in the appropriate places (you'll see them later).

```
homeView.collection = new MessageBoard()
homeView.collection.bind('refresh', homeView.render, homeView)
homeView.collection.fetch({
```

The `fetch` method will perform GET XHR request and it has `success` and `error` callbacks:

```
success: function(collection, response, options){
    console.log('Fetched ', collection)
```

The next line will trigger rendering only after all the messages are in the collection (and came from the server response):

```
            collection.trigger('refresh')
        },
        error: function(){
            console.error('Error fetching messages')
        }
    })
```

This event listener will be triggered by the SEND button as well as by the fetch. To avoid persisting existing records with message.save(), we add the check for the message.attributes._id. In other words, if this an existing message and it comes from the server (fetch), then it will have _id and we stop the execution flow. Otherwise, we persist the message and trigger rendering on success:

```
        homeView.collection.on('add', function(message) {
            if (message.attributes._id) return false
            message.save(null, {
                success: function(message) {
                    homeView.collection.trigger('refresh')
                    console.log('Saved ', message)
                },
                error: function(message) {
                    console.log('error')
                }
            })
        })
    },
```

The rest of the HomeView object is the same as in the 06-board-parse-sdk project. In the saveMessage we get the values of the username and the message text and add the new message object to the collection with collection.add(). This will call the event listener add, which we implemented in the initialize.

```
    saveMessage: function(){
        var newMessageForm = $('#new-message')
        var username = newMessageForm.find('[name="username"]').val()
        var message = newMessageForm.find('[name="message"]').val()
        this.collection.add({
            'username': username,
            'message': message
        })
    },
```

Last, we write or copy the render method that takes the template and the collection, then injects the resulting HTML into the element with ID content (this.el):

```
render: function() {
    console.log('Home view rendered')
    $(this.el).html(_.template(this.template)(this.collection))
}
})

app = new ApplicationRouter()
Backbone.history.start()
})
```

Here is the full source code of the 13-board-ui/app.js file (https://github.com/azat-co/fullstack-javascript/blob/master/13-board-ui/app.js):

```
var URL = 'http://localhost:1337/'
// var URL ='http://your-app-name.herokuapp.com/'

require([
    'libs/text!header.html',
    'libs/text!home.html',
    'libs/text!footer.html'],
    function (
        headerTpl,
        homeTpl,
        footerTpl) {

    var ApplicationRouter = Backbone.Router.extend({
        routes: {
            '': 'home',
            '*actions': 'home'
        },
        initialize: function() {
            this.headerView = new HeaderView()
            this.headerView.render()
            this.footerView = new FooterView()
            this.footerView.render()
        },
        home: function() {
            this.homeView = new HomeView()
            this.homeView.render()
        }
    })
```

```
HeaderView = Backbone.View.extend({
    el: '#header',
    templateFileName: 'header.html',
    template: headerTpl,
    initialize: function() {
    },
    render: function() {
        $(this.el).html(_.template(this.template))
    }
})

FooterView = Backbone.View.extend({
    el: '#footer',
    template: footerTpl,
    render: function() {
        this.$el.html(_.template(this.template))
    }
})
Message = Backbone.Model.extend({
    url: URL + 'messages/create.json'
})
MessageBoard = Backbone.Collection.extend ({
    model: Message,
    url: URL + 'messages/list.json'
})

HomeView = Backbone.View.extend({
    el: '#content',
    template: homeTpl,
    events: {
        'click #send': 'saveMessage'
    },

    initialize: function() {
        this.collection = new MessageBoard()
        this.collection.bind('all', this.render, this)
        this.collection.fetch()
        this.collection.on('add', function(message) {
            message.save(null, {
                success: function(message) {
                    console.log('saved ' + message)
                },
                error: function(message) {
                    console.log('error')
                }
            })
```

```
                console.log('saved' + message)
        })
    },
    saveMessage: function(){
        var newMessageForm=$('#new-message')
        var username=newMessageForm.find('[name="username"]').val()
        var message=newMessageForm.find('[name="message"]').val()
        this.collection.add({
            'username': username,
            'message': message
            })
    },
    render: function() {
        console.log(this.collection)
        $(this.el).html(_.template(this.template, this.collection))
    }
})

app = new ApplicationRouter()
Backbone.history.start()
})
```

This is it. For your reference, the front-end app source code is at https://github.com/ azat-co/fullstack-javascript/tree/master/13-board-u in the GitHub folder. I won't list it here because we had only a few changes comparing with the Parse SDK project. The next piece of the puzzle is the back end.

Message Board API

Supplemental video which walks you through the implementation and demonstrates the project: http://bit.ly/1QnsvEb.

The back-end Node.js application source code is at https://github.com/azat-co/ fullstack-javascript/tree/master/14-board-api in the GitHub folder, which has this structure:

```
/14-board-api
    -web.js
    -Procfile
    -package.json
```

The Procfile is for the Heroku deployment, and the package.json is for project metadata as well as for Hekoru deployment.

The web.js file is very similar to the 12-board-api-mongo, but has CORS headers and OPTIONS request handler code. The file starts with importation of dependencies:

```
var http = require('http')
var util = require('util')
var querystring = require('querystring')
var client = require('mongodb').MongoClient
```

Then we set the MongoDB connection string:

```
var uri = process.env.MONGOLAB_URI || 'mongodb://@127.0.0.1:27017/messages'
//MONGOLAB_URI=mongodb://user:pass@server.mongohq.com:port/db_name
```

We connect to the database using the string and client.connect method. It's important to handle the error and finish the execution flow with return if there's an error:

```
client.connect(uri, function(error, db) {
  if (error) return console.error(error)
```

After we are sure that there were no errors (otherwise the execution flow won't come to the next line), we select the collection, which is messages in this case:

```
  var collection = db.collection('messages')
```

The server code follows. We create the server instance and set up the origin variable based on the information from the request. This value will be in the Access-Control-Allow-Origin. The idea is that the response will have the value of the client's URL:

```
  var app = http.createServer(function (request, response) {
    var origin = (request.headers.origin || '*')
```

Check for the HTTP method verb. If it's OPTIONS, which we must implement for CORS, we start writing headers to the response object:

```
    if (request.method == 'OPTIONS') {
      response.writeHead('204', 'No Content', {
        'Access-Control-Allow-Origin': origin,
```

The next header will tell what methods are supported:

```
        'Access-Control-Allow-Methods':
          'GET, POST, PUT, DELETE, OPTIONS',
        'Access-Control-Allow-Headers': 'content-type, accept',
        'Access-Control-Max-Age': 10, // In seconds
        'Content-Length': 0
      })
      response.end()
```

175

We are done with OPTIONS, but we still need to implement GET and POST:

```
} else if (request.method === 'GET' && request.url ===
'/messages/list.json') {
  collection.find().toArray(function(error,results) {
    if (error) return console.error(error)
    var body = JSON.stringify(results)
```

We need to add a few headers to the response of the GET:

```
response.writeHead(200,{
  'Access-Control-Allow-Origin': origin,
  'Content-Type': 'text/plain',
  'Content-Length': body.length
})
console.log('LIST OF OBJECTS: ')
console.dir(results)
response.end(body)
})
```

Last but not least, we process POST:

```
} else if (request.method === 'POST' && request.url ===
'/messages/create.json') {
  request.on('data', function(data) {
    console.log('RECEIVED DATA:')
    console.log(data.toString('utf-8'))
```

We need to parse data to get the object so later we can save it into the database. The next line often causes bugs because front-end apps send data in one format and the server parses another. Please make sure to use the same format on the browser and server:

```
collection.insert(JSON.parse(data.toString('utf-8')),
{safe:true}, function(error, obj) {
  if (error) return console.error(error)
  console.log('OBJECT IS SAVED: ')
  console.log(JSON.stringify(obj))
  var body = JSON.stringify(obj)
```

We add the headers again. Maybe we should write a function and call it instead of writing the headers manually. Wait? Express.js is actually will do some of it for us but it's a topic of another book:

```
        response.writeHead(200,{
          'Access-Control-Allow-Origin': origin,
          'Content-Type': 'text/plain',
          'Content-Length': body.length
        })
        response.end(body)
      })
    })
  }
  })
  var port = process.env.PORT || 1337
  app.listen(port)
})
```

Here is a source code of web.js, our Node.js application implemented with CORS headers:

```
var http = require('http')
var util = require('util')
var querystring = require('querystring')
var client = require('mongodb').MongoClient

var uri = process.env.MONGOLAB_URI || 'mongodb://@127.0.0.1:27017/messages'
//MONGOLAB_URI = mongodb://user:pass@server.mongohq.com:port/db_name

client.connect(uri, function(error, db) {
  if (error) return console.error(error)
  var collection = db.collection('messages')
  var app = http.createServer(function (request, response) {
    var origin = (request.headers.origin || '*')
    if (request.method == 'OPTIONS') {
      response.writeHead('204', 'No Content', {
        'Access-Control-Allow-Origin': origin,
        'Access-Control-Allow-Methods':
          'GET, POST, PUT, DELETE, OPTIONS',
        'Access-Control-Allow-Headers': 'content-type, accept',
        'Access-Control-Max-Age': 10, // Seconds.
        'Content-Length': 0
      })
      response.end()
    } else if (request.method === 'GET' && request.url ===
    '/messages/list.json') {
```

```
      collection.find().toArray(function(error,results) {
        if (error) return console.error(error)
        var body = JSON.stringify(results)
        response.writeHead(200,{
          'Access-Control-Allow-Origin': origin,
          'Content-Type': 'text/plain',
          'Content-Length': body.length
        })
        console.log('LIST OF OBJECTS: ')
        console.dir(results)
        response.end(body)
      })
    } else if (request.method === 'POST' && request.url ===
    '/messages/create.json') {
      request.on('data', function(data) {
        console.log('RECEIVED DATA:')
        console.log(data.toString('utf-8'))
        collection.insert(JSON.parse(data.toString('utf-8')),
        {safe:true}, function(error, obj) {
          if (error) return console.error(error)
          console.log('OBJECT IS SAVED: ')
          console.log(JSON.stringify(obj))
          var body = JSON.stringify(obj)
          response.writeHead(200,{
            'Access-Control-Allow-Origin': origin,
            'Content-Type': 'text/plain',
            'Content-Length': body.length
          })
          response.end(body)
        })
      })
    }
  })
  var port = process.env.PORT || 1337
  app.listen(port)
})
```

Deployment to Heroku

Supplemental video which walks you through the implementation and demonstrates the project: http://bit.ly/1QnsvEb.

For your convenience, we have the front-end app at https://github.com/azat-co/fullstack-javascript/tree/master/13-board-ui and the back-end app with CORS is located at https://github.com/azat-co/fullstack-javascript/tree/master/14-board-api. By now, you probably know what to do, but as a reference, below are the steps to deploy these examples to Heroku.

We'll start with the API. In the `14-board-api` folder, execute the following code ($ `heroku login` is optional):

```
$ git init
$ git add .
$ git commit -am "first commit"
$ heroku login
$ heroku create
$ heroku addons:create mongolab:sandbox
$ git push heroku master
```

Watch the terminal messages. If the API is successfully deployed, you can test it with CURL or Postman. Then copy the URL from Heroku (e.g., `https://guarded-waters-1780.herokuapp.com`), and paste it into the `13-board-ui/app.js` file, assigning the value to the URL variable. Then, in the `13-board-ui` folder, execute:

```
$ git init
$ git add .
$ git commit -am "first commit"
$ heroku create
$ git push heroku master
$ heroku open
```

That's it. By now you should be able to see Message Board running in the cloud with UI (browser app) on one domain and API on another. In high-trafficked apps, the API will be hiding behind a load balancer so you can have multiple API servers on a single IP/URL. This way they'll hande more traffic and the system will become more resilient. You can take out, restart, or deploy on APIs one at a time with zero down time.

Same Domain Deployment Server

Supplemental video which walks you through the implementation and demonstrates the project: `http://bit.ly/1QnsvEb`.

Same domain deployment is *not recommended* for serious production applications, because static assets are better served with web servers like Nginx (not Node.js I/O engine), and separating API makes for less complicated testing, increased robustness, and quicker troubleshooting/monitoring. However, the same app/domain approach could be used for staging, testing, development environments, and/or tiny apps.

The idea is that API serves static files for the browser app as well, not just handling dynamic requests to its routes. So you can copy the 14-board-api code into a new folder 15-board-web. The beginning of the new server file is the same; we have GET and POST logic (this time CORS is not needed). The last condition in the chain of `if/else` needs to process the static files. Here's how we can do it.

```
...
  } else {
```

We use the url v0.11.0 module from https://github.com/defunctzombie/node-url to parse the path name from the URL. The path name is everything after the domain; for example, in http://webapplog.com/es6 the path name is /es6. This will be our folder and file names.

```
var uri = url.parse(request.url).pathname
```

It's good to have some logging to know that our system is working as it should:

```
console.log('Processing path: ', uri)
```

The next line deals with the root URI; that is, when you go to the web site and the path is empty or a slash. In this case, let's serve the index.html (if it exists):

```
if (uri == '' || uri == '/') uri = 'index.html'
```

The path.join() method will make this code cross-platform by creating a string with the proper slashes depending on the OS: that is, \ or / as separator. You can see the resulting path and file name in the logs:

```
filename = path.join(__dirname, staticFolder, uri)
console.log('Processing file: ', filename)
```

I always say never use synchronous functions in Node.js, unless you have to. This is such a case. Without the synch methods, we'll get racing conditions on our files meaning some will load faster than the others and cause conflicts:

```
stats = fs.statSync(filename)
if (error) {
  console.error(error)
```

Obviously, if the file doesn't exist we want to send 404 Not Found:

```
response.writeHead(404, {
  'Content-Type': 'text/plain'})
response.write('404 Not Found\n')
return response.end()
}
```

Let's make sure the requested resource is the file. If it's not the file, you can implement adding index.html as we did for the root. I don't have this code here. Our front-end app only needs to include files so this code will serve the files!

```
if(!stats.isFile()) {
  response.writeHead(404, {
    'Content-Type': 'text/plain'})
  response.write('404 Not Found\n')
  return response.end()
} else {
```

Finally, we read the file. We use the synchronous function again for the reasons mentioned above.

```
var file = fs.readFileSync(filename)
if (!file) {
  response.writeHead(500,
    {'Content-Type': 'text/plain'})
  response.write(err + '\n')
  return response.end()
}
```

I know that Douglas Crockford dislikes switch, but we'll use it here to determine the right content type for the response header. Most browsers will understand the content type okay if you omit the Content-Type header, but why not go an extra mile?

```
var extname = path.extname(filename)
var contentType = 'text/html'
switch (extname) {
    case '.js':
        contentType = 'text/javascript'
        break
    case '.css':
        contentType = 'text/css'
        break
    case '.json':
        contentType = 'application/json'
        break
    case '.png':
        contentType = 'image/png'
        break
    case '.jpg':
    case '.jpeg':
        contentType = 'image/jpg'
        break
    case '.wav':
        contentType = 'audio/wav'
        break
}
response.writeHead(200, {
  'Content-Type': contentType,
```

Another header that we send back with the response is Content-Length:

```
  'Content-Length': file.length
})
response.end(file)
  }
}
...
```

So this piece of code goes into the request handler of the server, which is inside of the database connect call. Just like the Russian Matreshka dolls. Confusing? Just refer to the full source code at https://github.com/azat-co/fullstack-javascript/tree/master/15-board-web.

Another, more elegant way is to use Node.js frameworks as Connect (http://www.senchalabs.org/connect/static.html), or Express (http://expressjs.com/en/index.html); because there is a special static middleware for JS and CSS assets. But those frameworks deserve a book on their own.

Now after you mastered basics of Node.js, MongoDB, Backbone.js, and Heroku, there's one bonus step to take. Check out the cloud solution Amazon Web Services known as EC2 (Infrastructure as a Service category of cloud computing).

Deployment to Amazon Web Services

Cloud is eating the world of computing. There are private and public clouds. AWS, probably the most popular choice among the public cloud offerings, falls under the IaaS category. The advantages of using an IaaS such as AWS over PaaS-like Heroku are as follows:

- It's more configurable (any services, packages, or operation systems).

- It's more controllable. There are no restrictions or limitations.

- It's cheaper to maintain. PaaS can quickly cost a fortune for high-performance resources.

In this tutorial, we'll be using 64-bit Amazon Linux AMI with CentOS (http://aws.amazon.com/amazon-linux-ami/).

Assuming you have your EC2 instance up and running, SSH into it and install all system updates with yum:

```
$ sudo yum update
```

You can try installing Node with yum. It should be available in the Extra Packages for Enterprise Linux repository (https://fedoraproject.org/wiki/EPEL):

```
$ sudo yum install nodejs npm --enablerepo=epel
```

This might take a while. Answer with y as the process goes. In the end, you should see something like this (your results may vary):

```
Installed:  nodejs.i686 0:0.10.26-1.el6        npm.noarch 0:1.3.6-4.
el6Dependency Installed:...Dependency Updated:...Complete!
```

You probably know this, but just in case, to check installations, type the following:

```
$ node -V$ npm -v
```

If the yum Node installation fails, see if you have EPEL (just see if the command below says epel):

```
$ yum repolist
```

If there's no epel, run:

```
$ rpm -Uvh http://download-i2.fedoraproject.org/pub/epel/6/i386/epel-
release-6-8.noarch.rpm
```

Then, try to install both Node.js and NPM again with:

```
$ sudo yum install nodejs npm --enablerepo=epel
```

Alternatively, you can compile Node from the source. To do so, install C++ compiler (again with yum):

```
$ sudo yum install gcc-c++ make
```

Same with openSSL:

```
$ sudo yum install openssl-devel
```

Then install Git with yum:

```
$ sudo yum install git
```

Finally, clone Node repository straight from GitHub:

```
$ git clone git://github.com/joyent/node.git
```

And build Node.js:

```
$ cd node
$ git checkout v0.10.12
$ ./configure
$ make
$ sudo make install
```

■ **Note**   For a different version of Node.js, you can list them all with $ `git tag -l` and checkout the one you need.

To install npm, run:

```
$ git clone https://github.com/isaacs/npm.git
$ cd npm
$ sudo make install
```

More information on using yum can be found at the following locations:

- Managing Software with yum (`https://www.centos.org/docs/5/html/yum/`)

- Installing Node.js via package managers (`https://github.com/nodejs/node-v0.x-archive/wiki/Installing-Node.js-via-package-manager`)

- Tips on securing your EC2 instance (`http://aws.amazon.com/articles/1233`)

Once you have Git and npm and Node, you are good to deploy your code (manually). Pull the code from the repository. You might need to provide credentials or upload your SSH keys to the AWS. Then start the Node server with pm2 (`https://github.com/Unitech/pm2`) or similar process manager (Figure 8-1). pm2 is good because it has a lot of features not only to keep the process running but also to scale it; it even has load balancing.

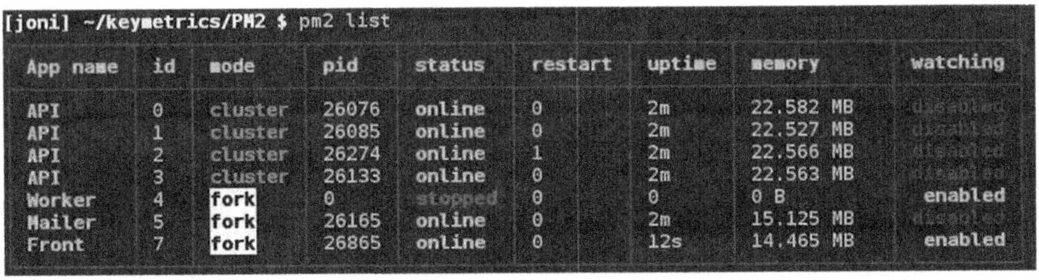

Figure 8-1. *pm2 running multiple Node processes*

To install pm2:

```
$ npm install pm2 -g
```

To start your application:

```
$ pm2 start app.js
```

To list all running processes:

```
$ pm2 list
```

That's pretty much all you need to do. Ideally you want to automate the deployment. Also, you might want to add some d.init or upstart scripts to launch your pm2 or another process manager automatically.

Steps for other OS on AWS are similar. You would use their package manager to install Node, Git, and npm, then get the code (Git or rsync) and launch it with the process manager. You don't need the process manager. You can launch with node itself, but it's better to use some process manager.

Now, while the Node.js app is running, executing $ netstat -apn | grep 80, the remote machine should show the process. For example, for a Node app listening on port 80:

```
tcp    0    0 0.0.0.0:80    0.0.0.0:*    LISTEN    1064/node
```

On the EC2 instance, either configure the firewall to redirect connections (e.g., port to Node.js 3000, but this is too advanced for our example) or disable the firewall (okay for our quick demonstration and development purposes):

```
$ service iptables save$ service iptables stop$ chkconfig iptables off
```

In the AWS console, find your EC2 instance and apply a proper rule to allow for inbound traffic, for example,

```
Protocol: TCPPort Range: 80Source: 0.0.0.0/0
```

And from your local machine, that is, your development computer, you can either use the public IP or the public DNS (the Domain Name System) domain, which is found and copied from the AWS console under that instance's description. For example,

```
$ curl XXX.XXX.XXX.XXX -v
```

It's worth mentioning that AWS supports many other operating systems via its AWS Marketplace (https://aws.amazon.com/marketplace). Although AWS EC2 is a very popular and affordable choice, there other alternatives as well: Joyent (https://www.joyent.com/), Windows Azure (https://azure.microsoft.com/en-us/), Rackspace Open Cloud (http://www.rackspace.com/cloud), and others.

Summary

This chapter deals with descriptions of different deployment approaches, the final version of Message Board application, and its deployment with two approaches: different and the same domains. We covered deployment using the Git and Heroku command-line interfaces to deploy to PaaS. And we worked through examples of installing and building a Node.js environment on AWS EC2 and running Node.js apps on AWS with CentOS.

APPENDIX A

Conclusion and Further Reading

This appendix provides the book's conclusion, lists of JavaScript blog posts, articles, e-books, books, and other resources.

Conclusion

We hope you've enjoyed this book. It was intended to be small on theory but big on practice and give you an overview of multiple technologies, frameworks, and techniques used in modern agile web development. Full Stack JavaScript touched topics such as the following:

- jQuery, JSON, and AJAX/XHR
- Twitter Bootstrap, CSS, and LESS
- Backbone.js, AMD, and Require.js
- Node.js, REST API, and Parse.com
- MongoDB and BSON
- AWS, Heroku, and MongoLab

If you need in-depth knowledge or references, scroll down to the list of suggested reading or do a Google search.

Practical aspects included building multiple versions of the Message Board app:

- jQuery + Parse.com JS REST API
- Backbone and Parse.com JS SDK
- Backbone and Node.js
- Backbone and Node.js + MongoDB

The Message Board application has all the foundation of a typical web/mobile application: fetching data, displaying it, submitting new data. Other examples include:

- jQuery + OpenWeatherMap RESP API

- Parse.com "Save John"

- Node.js "Hello World"

- MongoDB "Print Collections"

- Backbone.js "Hello World"

- Backbone.js "Apple Database"

Please submit a GitHub issue if you have any feedback; comments; suggestions; or you've found typos, bugs, mistakes, or other errata: `https://github.com/azat-co/` `fullstack-javascript/issues`.

Other ways to connect are via: @azat_co (`http://twitter.com/azat_co`), `http://webapplog.com`, `http://azat.co`.

In case you enjoyed Node.js and want to find out more about building production web services with Express.js—a de factor standard for Node.js web apps—take a look at my book Pro Express.js.

Further Reading

Here is a list of resources, courses, books, and blogs for further reading.

JavaScript Resources and Free E-Books

- ES6 Cheatsheet (`https://gumroad.com/l/LDwVU/git-1CC81D40`)

- MongoDB and Mongoose Cheatsheet
  (`https://gumroad.com/l/mongodb/git-874e6fb4`)

- Express.js 4 Cheatsheet
  (`https://gumroad.com/l/NQiQ/git-874E6FB4`)

- React Cheatsheet
  (`https://gumroad.com/l/IJRtw/git-FB2C5E22`)

- JavaScript For Cats (`http://jsforcats.com/`): an introduction for new programmers

- Eloquent JavaScript (`http://eloquentjavascript.net/`): a modern introduction to programming

- Superhero.js (`http://superherojs.com/`): comprehensive collection of JS resources

- JavaScript Guide (`https://developer.mozilla.org/en-US/` `docs/Web/JavaScript/Guide`) by Mozilla Developer Network

- JavaScript Reference (https://developer.mozilla.org/en-US/docs/Web/JavaScript/Reference) by Mozilla Developer Network

- Why Use Closure (http://howtonode.org/why-use-closure): practical uses of a closure in event-based programming

- Prototypal Inheritance (http://howtonode.org/prototypical-inheritance): objects with inherited and local properties

- Control Flow in Node (http://howtonode.org/control-flow): parallel vs. serial flows

- Truthy and Falsey Values (http://docs.nodejitsu.com/articles/javascript-conventions/what-are-truthy-and-falsy-values)

- How to Write Asynchronous Code (http://docs.nodejitsu.com/articles/getting-started/control-flow/how-to-write-asynchronous-code)

- Smooth CoffeeScript (http://autotelicum.github.io/Smooth-CoffeeScript/): free interactive HTML5 book and collection of quick references and other goodies

- Developing Backbone.js Applications (http://addyosmani.com/backbone-fundamentals/): free early release book By Addy Osmani and O'Reilly

- Step by step from jQuery to Backbone (https://github.com/kjbekkelund/writings/blob/master/published/understanding-backbone.md)

- Open Web Platform Daily Digest (http://daily.w3viewer.com/): JS daily digest

- DISTILLED HYPE (http://distilledhype.net/): JS blog/newsletter

JavaScript Books

- JavaScript: The Good Parts (http://shop.oreilly.com/product/9780596517748.do)

- JavaScript: The Definitive Guide (http://www.amazon.com/dp/0596101996/?tag=stackoverfl08-20)

- Secrets of the JavaScript Ninja (http://www.manning.com/resig/)

- Pro JavaScript Techniques (http://www.amazon.com/dp/1590597273/?tag=stackoverfl08-20)

Node.js Resources and Free E-Books

- Felix's Node.js Beginners Guide (`http://nodeguide.com/beginner.html`)

- Felix's Node.js Style Guide (`http://nodeguide.com/style.html`)

- Felix's Node.js Convincing the boss guide (`http://nodeguide.com/convincing_the_boss.html`)

- Introduction to NPM (`http://howtonode.org/introduction-to-npm`)

- NPM Cheatsheet (`http://blog.nodejitsu.com/npm-cheatsheet`)

- Interactive Package.json Cheatsheet (`http://package.json.nodejitsu.com`)

- Official Node.js Documentation (`http://nodejs.org/api`)

- Node Guide (`http://nodeguide.com`)

- Node Tuts (`http://nodetuts.com`)

- What Is Node? (`http://www.amazon.com/What-Is-Node-ebook/dp/B005ISQ7JC`): free Kindle edition

- Mastering Node.js (`http://visionmedia.github.com/masteringnode`): open source node ebook

- Mixu's Node book (`http://book.mixu.net`): A book about using Node.js

- Learn Node.js Completely and with Confidence (`http://javascriptissexy.com/learn-node-js-completely-and-with-confidence`): guide to learning JavaScript in 2 weeks

- How to Node (`http://howtonode.org`): The zen of coding in node.js

Node.js Books

- The Node Beginner Book (`https://leanpub.com/nodebeginner`)

- Hands-on Node.js (`https://leanpub.com/hands-on-nodejs`)

- Backbone Tutorials (`https://leanpub.com/backbonetutorials`)

- Smashing Node.js (`http://www.amazon.com/Smashing-Node-js-JavaScript-Everywhere-Magazine/dp/1119962595`)

- The Node Beginner Book (`http://www.nodebeginner.org`)

- Hands-on Node.js (`http://nodetuts.com/handson-nodejs-book.html`)

- Node: Up and Running (`http://shop.oreilly.com/product/0636920015956.do`)
- Node.js in Action (`http://www.manning.com/cantelon`)
- Node: Up and Running (`http://www.amazon.com/Node-Running-Scalable-Server-Side-JavaScript/dp/1449398588`): Scalable Server-Side Code with JavaScript
- Node Web Development (`http://www.amazon.com/Node-Web-Development-David-Herron/dp/184951514X`): A practical introduction to Node
- Node Cookbook (`http://www.amazon.com/Node-Cookbook-David-Mark-Clements/dp/1849517185`)
- Pro Express.js (`http://proexpressjs.com`)
- Practical Node.js (`http://practicalnodebook.com`)
- Deep Express.js API Reference (`http://amzn.to/1xcHanf`)

Interactive Online Classes and Courses

- Cody Academy (`http://www.codecademy.com`): interactive programming courses
- Programr (`http://www.programr.com`)
- LearnStreet (`http://www.learnstreet.com`)
- Treehouse (`http://teamtreehouse.com`)
- lynda.com (`http://www.lynda.com`): software, creative and business courses
- Udacity (`https://www.udacity.com`): Massive open online courses
- Coursera (`https://www.coursera.org`)

Startup Books and Blogs

- Hackers & Painters (`http://www.amazon.com/Hackers-Painters-Big-Ideas-Computer/dp/1449389554`)
- The Lean Startup (`http://theleanstartup.com/book`)
- The Startup Owner's Manual (`http://www.amazon.com/Startup-Owners-Manual-Step-Step/dp/0984999302`)
- The Entrepreneur's Guide to Customer Development (`http://www.amazon.com/The-Entrepreneurs-Guide-Customer-Development/dp/0982743602`)
- Venture Hacks (`http://venturehacks.com`)
- Webapplog (`http://webapplog.com`)

Index

Get the eBook for only $5!

Why limit yourself?

Now you can take the weightless companion with you wherever you go and access your content on your PC, phone, tablet, or reader.

Since you've purchased this print book, we're happy to offer you the eBook in all 3 formats for just $5.

Convenient and fully searchable, the PDF version enables you to easily find and copy code—or perform examples by quickly toggling between instructions and applications. The MOBI format is ideal for your Kindle, while the ePUB can be utilized on a variety of mobile devices.

To learn more, go to www.apress.com/companion or contact support@apress.com.

Apress®
THE EXPERT'S VOICE™

All Apress eBooks are subject to copyright. All rights are reserved by the Publisher, whether the whole or part of the material is concerned, specifically the rights of translation, reprinting, reuse of illustrations, recitation, broadcasting, reproduction on microfilms or in any other physical way, and transmission or information storage and retrieval, electronic adaptation, computer software, or by similar or dissimilar methodology now known or hereafter developed. Exempted from this legal reservation are brief excerpts in connection with reviews or scholarly analysis or material supplied specifically for the purpose of being entered and executed on a computer system, for exclusive use by the purchaser of the work. Duplication of this publication or parts thereof is permitted only under the provisions of the Copyright Law of the Publisher's location, in its current version, and permission for use must always be obtained from Springer. Permissions for use may be obtained through RightsLink at the Copyright Clearance Center. Violations are liable to prosecution under the respective Copyright Law.

Printed in the United States
By Bookmasters